Think Well, Live Well Now

Change Your Thoughts and Transform Your Life!

Benay Behnke

Copyright © 2011 by Benay Behnke

Think Well, Live Well Now
Change Your Thoughts, and Transform Your Life!
by Benay Behnke

Printed in the United States of America

ISBN 9781612157849

All rights reserved solely by the author. The author guarantees all contents are original and do not infringe upon the legal rights of any other person or work. No part of this book may be reproduced in any form without the permission of the author. The views expressed in this book are not necessarily those of the publisher.

Unless otherwise indicated, Bible quotations are taken from The King James Version. Copyright © 2003 by Thomas Nelson; and The Amplified Bible. Copyright © 1954, 1958, 1962, 1964, 1965, 1987 by the Zondervan Corporation and the Lockman Foundation.

Edited by: Jim Kochenburger

www.xulonpress.com

Table of Contents

Chapter 1 - My Story: The Writing of This Book.........................15
Chapter 2 - Invisible Thoughts Grow Trees................................22
Chapter 3 - How Thoughts Are Processed Physiologically...........35
Chapter 4 - The Heart has Intelligence 51
Chapter 5 - Imagination 59
Chapter 6 - The Battle for the Heart 66
Chapter 7 - Do Genes Control Us 74
Chapter 8 - Activating Your Heart Intelligence 77
Chapter 9 - How Separate Are We..82
Chapter 10 - You Are a Transmitter and a Receiver 92
Chapter 11 - Thoughts Originate from Two Energy Systems.....107
Chapter 12 - Guard Your Heart...116
Chapter 13 - It Isn't In Your Genes...122
Chapter 14 - Has Quantum Physics Found God's Energy?.........133
Chapter 15 - Perception Deceptions 147
Chapter 16 - Cells Store Memory 171
Chapter 17 - Confessions Create Reality....................................176
Chapter 18 - Faith is Incubated...198
Chapter 19 - You are a Generator...206
Chapter 20 – Trust Keeps Faith Incubating 218
Chapter 21 - Be Transformed..228

Introduction

There is...
    One thing that no one can take from you.
One thing that no one can do for you.
One thing that is invisible when you do it.
One thing that causes everything to come together for you or tears down what you have built.
One thing you do without knowing you are doing it.
One thing that changes who you are every second, yet you don't even know it.
One thing that causes you to be in poverty or financial riches.
One thing that keeps you healthy and whole or causes you to be sick and die.

Everything seen comes from a direct connection to what's invisible — your thoughts. Therefore, what you think has the power to literally transform your life. This is a book to help you transform your life.

Your life is what your thoughts make it. James Allen wrote "*As a Man Thinketh*" in 1903 and inspired a list of self-help writers including Napoleon Hill, Dale Carnegie and Norman Vincent Peale. One key thing is different between then and now — science has discovered what the word of God has said for thousands of years. In these pages you will learn what science has discovered up to now and how the word of God makes science more believable.

James Allen also observed that a person "will find that as he alters his thoughts toward things and other people, things and other people will alter towards him." (*As a Man Thinketh*) This is the basic premise of the Law of Attraction. In these pages, you will come to understand what God's Word says about this and the science of the law.

The Law of Attraction is based on the principle that what we focus on in thought will attract into our lives whatever energy we exchanged in the process because everything seen and unseen is comprised of energy. The energy that is generated by our unseen thoughts attracts or repels the energy matter of what we ultimately see and experience as a result.

This is found in the discoveries of quantum physics. Nothing in the universe is in a fixed or stationary condition at all times because all matter is vibrating energy which responds to our thoughts. This is why the word, in Hebrews 11:3b says, "what we see was not made out of things which are visible" (AMP). This is also the essence of faith, "the substance of things hoped for, the evidence of things not seen" (Hebrews 11:1, KJV).

This book isn't New Age but rather Old Age. The Law of Attraction is a spiritual law of God that New Age has basically taken and perverted to take the emphasis off of God to place it on "self." The source of all energy is God; nothing is "self"-made. There is no created thing that has greater power than its original Creator, including Satan. God spoke and everything became and still becomes because of the energy that is in Him.

Everything you see began as invisible motion. Genesis tells us that God spoke the earth into existence. God spoke His thoughts. The source of all energy and all matter is the mind of God.

Thoughts are mental energy in which you invest your mind either positively or negatively. There is a mental exchange of energies that take place when you meditate, dwell on, or invest your attention upon and what you speak about. This type of investing in our mind results directly, either positively or negatively.

Your soul forms attachments to whatever it can conceive in your thought process. Our souls can become attached to our children, husband, wife, friends, pets, stuff, and so on—by how we think.

Thoughts are currents of electricity that create electromagnetic fields connecting positive or negative charges.

What's more amazing is that you don't just have thoughts or think with your brain—your heart thinks as well. Proverbs 4:23 says, "Keep and guard your heart with all vigilance and above all that you guard, for out of it flow the springs of life." Positive thoughts attract positive attachments; negative thoughts attract negative attachments. Energy exchanges can be intentional and unintentional; conscious and non-conscious.

Sometimes we are completely oblivious to what we've attached ourselves by not realizing that we have focused for too long on something in our mind. I believe this is why we are told in 2 Corinthians 10:5b to take every thought captive, "bringing into captivity every thought to the obedience of Christ." (KJV)

Whatever you think is hidden in the innermost chambers of your thought life will, sooner or later, be brought into the light for the world to see. First Corinthians 4:5 states that God "He will both bring to light the secret things that are [now hidden] in darkness and disclose and expose the [secret] aims (motives and purposes) of hearts" (AMP). There are seeds in the heart that get spoken by the mouth and produce a crop. Luke 6:45 provides a mouth full about this: "A good man out of the good treasure of his heart bringeth forth that which is good; and an evil man out of the evil treasure of his heart bringeth forth that which is evil: for of the abundance of the heart his mouth speaketh." Everything that you see began as a seed thought.

Each of us produces a crop for the physical realm has its seeds in the spiritual. These seeds are watered, fertilized, given light (or not)—all to produce a crop. Grabbing hold of this profound spiritual truth allows you to activate the right connections that can transform your life. What happens in the physical realm is what is happening in the invisible spiritual realm, which is the "causal realm." Invisible motion of spiritual things is what engineers, molds and forms the current and future state of your life. This is knowledge you must possess to grasp and harness the massive power of your thoughts, words, ideas, and even your prayers.

What exists for you comes from the inside out. If you want to possess the promises of God, you must first take possession of your thoughts. By taking possession of them, you will be able to take control of your life. Have you ever felt like life was running you? You just didn't realize that you were allowing this. One ends up becoming a slave to life's circumstances non-consciously due to strongholds held in the mind.

Your health, success and prosperity depend upon what happens in your thoughts. To transform your thoughts, you must first gain knowledge of how powerful they are, how they cause things to happen in your body (physically), and then dictate your circumstances.

The second thing to do is to apply that knowledge to cause a change in your thoughts, which puts you in greater control than your previous thoughts allowed. God wants you to live a life of abundance, not one of defeat and lack. It is His desire to give you divine health, success, and prosperity. Third John 1:2 says this, "Beloved, I wish above all things that thou mayest prosper and be in health, even as thy soul prospereth." God's desire is that you walk in your destiny and that you will "by loving" your life.

Lance Wallnau teaches in his *Personal Mastery* course that there is a point of convergence that God wired us to walk in. Convergence is the sweet spot. It's when God gives you a role that matches how you were neurologically wired. Your signature strengths are the core gifts and talents God gave you to accomplish the role He has for you. When you engage your fully developed gifts and talents is when you experience fulfillment, that's your passion pulse. It's when your gifts and talents have tapped into your signature strengths and you are a hundred percent alive with passion. When you are walking in convergence you are doing what you were gifted to do and you have a sense of euphoria doing it.

Every thought holds a picture. When I say "elephant" you see an image in your mind of an elephant. Man begins with a thought and builds upon that thought by mulling it over in the mind, reviewing a series of images. That process forms a complete picture of something he believes he is able to accomplish. Then he joins his will to the thoughts of his imagination, causing the power of observation with an expectancy to bring it from the invisible energy of the mind into the visible physical world.

Many sources quote Einstein as having said, "I am enough of an artist to draw freely upon my imagination. Imagination is more than knowledge. Knowledge is limited. Imagination encircles the world." Imagination drives the engine of innovation, discovery, problem solving, and peacemaking. Einstein understood that whatever can be imagined already exists; it simply exists in another dimension, in another form or substance that transforms by our thought processes. This is in essence what faith is.

The quality of your life is directly connected to the quality of your thoughts. Your thoughts determine who you are, what you are, how and where you live, where you go in life, what you get from life, who and what you love to spend time with, your identity, what you accomplish, what you change or don't change, and so on.

You will never have more, go further, or accomplish greater things than your thoughts will allow you. Change your thoughts and change your world. Your life is a reflection of your thoughts. When you meditate on success, you live a successful life.

Take the Limits off Your Mind

This book will help you understand many things about yourself that you never knew before and will reveal how they have been affecting the quality of your life. This is a book to both read and a book to "work" what you read. I recommend that you journal as you read and work this book.

Every bit of information in this book was directed into my life by the Holy Spirit. My knowledge of this caused me to see things totally differently than ever before in my life. As I received these downloads from the Holy Spirit and wrote this book, the divine knowledge I gleaned has transformed me and renewed my mind. This is the challenge of renewing the mind—you have to open the spiritual channels of your mind so that God can download divine knowledge and divine thoughts into your brain.

You are not reading this book by coincidence, or by accident. There are divinely appointed times for everything. There is a reason that this book is just for you at this time. Mankind is sicker than ever before. New diseases are being discovered and labeled at increasing rates. Technology is developing so rapidly that by the time a computer is bought, it is already outdated. The computer that will make that new computer of yours obsolete has already been developed and is nearly ready for the market. We are living in a time when knowledge, in general, is increasing at multiplied rates over the past; so much so, that it's hard to keep up. Yet with all this knowledge, why are we less and less equipped to handle what life seems to hand out? After all, isn't experience supposed to teach us what we need to learn? Or is there more to it than that? Yes, there is more to it, and in these pages, I will tell you what it is.

I propose that it isn't only new experiences that serve as our teacher, but rather a transformation of the mind. What do I mean by that? Do we know where our mind really is? Do we know where thoughts truly come from and where they reside? What is causing this rapidly moving, invisible motion? You may be surprised at the answers to these questions.

Pastor Fiona Des Fontaine, senior pastor of His Church in South Africa, had some good thoughts about the Israelite's in one of her sermons about transformation of the mind. I am paraphrasing what she taught. To experience something, no matter how miraculous, does not necessarily transform your life. Why? In addition to that experience there must be a deliverance that takes place in the mind and the heart. The word of God, when spoken, causes transformation, not experiences. All the miracles that Jesus performed didn't stop Him from being crucified. Miracles don't convince people that God is a good God.

Consider the Israelite's and Moses. Something in their brains never transformed. It is one thing to experience a deliverance; quite another to be transformed. Every crisis produced a complaint from the Israelite's towards Moses because something in their thinking never got hold of the truth that God was good and would provide and take care of them. The crisis didn't inspire faith in them either. Why? They didn't believe that God had their best interest at heart or that He had a plan that was good for them.

Are things much different today? Could this apply to us today? The Israelite's expected God to let them down time and time again, which is why they complained over and over, even when they saw signs, wonders, and miracles from God.

The Israelite's followed Moses instead of God. When Moses went up the mountain to meet with God in Exodus 32, it only took the Israelite's six weeks to build a golden calf, a visible image, or idol. They wanted a god they could see with their natural eyes, who would be in their physical presence at all times when they needed him to do something. Are the majority of us much different today?

It is a fact that our minds can remain in captivity even after our bodies have been set free. You can even experience a healing in your body—yet your mind remains untransformed. Could this be the reason as many as ninety percent of people who receive healing at revivals or crusades lose their healing? This idea has been mentioned in various sources and if even remotely accurate is very disheartening. What is the reason for this? Our thinking must be transformed, not just our physical bodies delivered. Where your mind goes, your body follows. The mind must be renewed. It must take hold of the Word in order for that healing to hold. A person can receive healing but his mind can remain captive, which usually results in another crisis—under which he collapses. So it was with the people when they no longer saw Moses. So it was with Jesus. When he ascended to heaven in his heavenly body and the people could no longer see Him physically—they drifted away from Him. They experienced a physical deliverance but their minds were never transformed.

Experiencing deliverance is not the same as being transformed. Most miracles of deliverance follow that pattern—when the deliverer leaves, people lose their deliverances. We must learn to sustain our deliverances from life's circumstances by knowing and looking to God, whom we learn to trust with the knowledge of His word.

When you must see everything with the five senses in order to receive what you need, you are a candidate for transformation by the Word in your mind. We do not exercise faith if we receive what we already have or that with which we are already familiar. Get prepared to expand your thinking and to take the limits off!

Chapter 1

My Story: The Writing of This Book

Everyone's life will tell a story, but how many make it one worth reading? By sharing some of my story from the last four years, I believe you will get a greater understanding of why and how this book came into being.

I lost my job, without warning, in February 2007. Little did I know that God would place a radical expectation and calling upon my life that would transform me from the inside out. Moments after being told I had no job, God told me this was a good thing and that I would never work a conventional job again. My world suddenly became completely different from anything I had ever known before.

To my concern about where I would find my "money tree" without a conventional job, God called me to walk by faith like never before in my life. How long would this season last I wondered. In another season of my life I thought I might lose my son. (I almost lost my own life through physical abuse.) I almost lost my house in a previous faith walk. Would I need to walk in an altogether different forest than ever before?

I don't know about you but I don't enjoy not being able to see the trees for the forest. I felt like I was whisked away and dropped right into the Amazon Rainforest. I could see nothing but earth, trees, and things I could not recognize. The forest was so thick; I couldn't even see the sky when I looked up. Do you get the picture? Have you been there yourself? Then you know how uncomfortable the surroundings are.

The first thing I did after walking out of my ex-workplace was I call my one and only son, Norby, to tell him what happened. Being single, I turned to the only family I had that was close to me for a word of comfort, and that was Norby. After listening to me for a moment, he said to me, "Mom, I think this is a good thing." (Now where had I heard that already?) Either he knew something I didn't or God was speaking to me through him, because he was confirming the "crazy" thought God had given me moments earlier.

This started what I have come to call, a radical sabbatical. (Warning: Do not try this unless you know that you know you have heard from God—and that it isn't a false dream.) When God tells you that you aren't going to work a conventional job again, that is pretty radical. Trust me, I tested myself mercilessly: Had I not heard quite right? But I noticed over time, that each time I would go out to seek a job, I would become physically ill. When I quit trying to look for a job, I would have a great peace come over me and settle on me. After trying this a few times for the first year, (yes you read that right, the first year), I knew I was doing what He wanted me to do. When I began this journey, I expected it to last only a few months, no longer than six. As I am writing this, I am still in this radical sabbatical and know it will end when I finish writing this book.

Let me emphasize again, this journey is not a call for everyone's life, but it has been my call. What I thought would last for only a few months has now lasted almost four years, as of February, 2011. Trust me; I did not have a lot to sustain me over this time. I am no "rich young ruler" (the one Jesus told to give all he had to the poor—and then to follow Him). But I have learned what it is like to have, and to "have not" due to giving it all away to follow Jesus where He wanted me to go, or investing it in materials that teach about His Kingdom. I also know what it is like to have the Lord take care of my needs when I am in need. This has happened more than once in my life and He has always come through for me—and He always will.

I have been transformed by the renewing of my mind personally, which is what qualifies me to be used to challenge others to do the same. I am a spiritual scientist. I want to know why something is or is not happening in life. However, I will say this has been the most radical faith experience of my life—one I continue to this day.

Many of those who know me will read this for the first time and likely say, "I didn't know she hasn't received any income from a job, all this time." Most would ask how I've made it! But, I have learned to trust God for provision to follow the vision. He builds a testimony through us if we will let Him. I know without a doubt that whatever God calls you to do, He will also provide for you to do it. Where He leads, He provides. It often isn't in our timing of when we think we need it. Our job is to be obedient along the journey. Obedience is better than sacrifice.

During this time, people ask me, "What do you do?" I typically say I am between jobs, or I am studying for something God has for me, but I would not volunteer much information. Rather than putting up with the "you must be crazy" looks, I used wisdom and kept my mouth shut. (No matter what I answered I knew a good many people in the world would look at me as if I was a misfit. According to the world system I was a misfit in that I did not live in the way most people do.) I have been living in a place that is not of this world, but in a different "dimension," a foreign land.

I wouldn't blame people if they thought me a little odd, or as a misfit—before this journey, I might have thought the same thing of someone, had I discovered they hadn't worked for months (or years). It is the way we have come to attach people's identity to what they do "in" this world, instead of to what God created and planned for them to "be" for Him in this world. The real question should be not what you "do" but what you should "be." In being who you were designed to be, you discover hidden secret things you never knew about.

God started to teach me, as I gave Him my days to study whatever He led me to learn about, just as if I were working eight to twelve hours a day at a conventional job. Only thing was, I was enrolled in the school of the Holy Spirit.

You may ask how I knew what to study for that many hours. I just started listening and following the Holy Spirit for whatever He would tell me to do, listen to, or read. All teaching included the word of God. I discovered that what He started to unpack in me was everything that I had a love for, but had never known before. I ate it up—even physics! I had struggled to pass science in high school.

In college psychology courses, I had studied the brain and loved it the most. He expanded on that love these many years later. He took me into biology and physiology of the body. A year ago, I began to help people who were in pain and sick through therapy, prayer and using biofeedback. Biofeedback is a big word for using a device to detect ultrasounds in the body that are out of balance and causing illness, and then provide therapy to bring the body back into proper balances. This is America and I don't make any claims for treatments of illnesses. God makes the difference in every part of life.

The biofeedback device was not cheap, nor was the nine months of training in its therapeutic use. I was able to practice on people to learn how to use it. There were many successful results, including those for my grandson, Dustin Blane and I. I was healed of chronic pain due to a badly deteriorated L5 disc in my spine. (I had been in pain with every movement.) I am now pain free, after eleven years of that constant pain. It wasn't until months later that I realized my healing didn't come entirely from a method. I noticed my thinking had changed and I knew it had to do with my manifested healing.

My grandson had been experiencing the symptoms of Lyme disease. He was a sickly child from birth but really developed great challenges just over the past three years. Today he has none of the major symptoms, including respiratory failure. There were other wonderful stories of illnesses and pain going away, but after about a year and all the time I had invested into what I thought would become a practice and teaching clinic opportunity for me, I sensed God was moving me on. He caused me to feel uneasy and told me He wanted me to spend more intense time with Him again. So the use of the ultrasound was put on hold as I dove back into the study of how the spirit affects our physiology, in terms of our health and what we deal with in life.

When I began studying physiology, God told me to look for the root "cause" of disease and illness. Yet, when I thought I had found the method He led me to (using the biofeedback and ultrasound device to help discover the causes of physical and mental illness),

He told me I still had not uncovered the root cause of disease. Being a spiritual scientist I was driven to seek more revelation.

This is when the Lord started to bring all the pieces together. For three years God had downloaded to me before I could see the clear picture of what He was doing in my life. This is the frustration we experience with God sometimes. When He says He is going to give us a word, we want at least a paragraph, if not the whole book, not just a word.

What we don't realize is that if He gave us the whole book about who He created us to be and what He wants to reveal through us, we would run from it because it would be too hard for us to believe. It takes time to develop into who He created us to be. It took a short nine months for us to physically develop before our entrance into this world; it takes a lifetime to get to develop all that we were designed to be. Case in point, He told me over a year's time, by way of three different people, that I would write a book. I protested that I did not know how to write a book; I was not an author. The problem is that we don't know what we are capable of if we continue to try things by our "self."

I had an interest in physics because of what I found that quantum physics had discovered. Everywhere I turned, I realized that what they found, and couldn't completely explain with logical sense, was what the Bible talked about. (I won't go into detail because, as you read this book, you will know exactly what I mean as I share all that has been revealed to me.) Needless to say, my jaw would drop as I discovered things through science that caused the word of God to make literal sense to me.

Allow God to Unpack What He Put in You

We never know what we are capable of because we don't know who we are until we allow God to unpack that which He put in us. I had no idea why I loved physics. It began to make sense to me when He started to show me who He is, where He is, and just how literal His word is, because of what quantum physics has discovered. I started seeing the real meaning for "why" God told us to do things in His word; so we would experience well-being in life and be able to overcome every obstacle we encounter.

Before being transformed, what didn't make sense to me was if I accepted the word by faith and hope, I could somehow do what it said. You will discover as you read this book, that things were said by God for literal, physical reasons that make sense. We can understand God's word better today than ever before because science has revealed what the Word has always told us.

When I started to be transformed I found more of God and I started to find myself! That's the irony of it. The other irony of this journey has been that as I look back on these past three years and all the downloads I went through to be able to write this book, I realized that I was being transformed by the knowledge of Him whom I was discovering. Science is tied to what the word of God says He is. The word that says, "My people perish for a lack of knowledge," is more literal then I thought.

Everything you read in this book has been my personal discovery. The personal discovery came as a result of the Holy Spirit guiding my steps to discover who God the Father and Jesus are. Through this journey, I found Him in new ways I never intended to. He unexpectedly revealed me, unpacking all that had been in me all along. It transformed me and my mind was renewed as a result of seeking Him and what He wanted to reveal to me. He is the only one who can reveal who we are to us.

Among His other names, He is also Jehovah "Sneaky." I thought I was writing a book when He told me that I was being transformed in the process. This didn't come to my understanding until two months ago, after I had been writing for seven months and kept planning to complete writing every two weeks.

After saying that I would finish in two weeks for the fourth or fifth time, I had a friend tell me that I wouldn't finish writing until I "became the message of the book." That took me aback. I realized that it was the truth. I was being transformed by what I was writing in the book, as I received revelation from God.

Everything in this book, every bit of knowledge I've gained, has changed me. This is not by accident because once we are healed and transformed; we then possess the "legal," legitimate right to teach others to receive their transformation. How exciting! We are never given gifts to keep for ourselves; they are all meant to be shared with others. I share all that is within this book with all of you who will read it and hear what it is imparting to you.

This book will transform your life, if you will receive the knowledge and understanding of the Word that is in it.

Science has caught up with explaining the Scriptures as never before in history, yet we hear little about this. I had an intense desire to "know" God at the core of His being, as best as my finite mind would allow for that understanding and knowledge. You may be surprised, as I was, to find that science has found God in everything.

Even as early as fifty years ago, Einstein found God's energy of light in everything. There was an unexplainable energy force found in his mathematical blackboards. Gerald Feinberg, a young scientist who studied the blackboards of Einstein's formulas, found a subatomic particle that moves faster than the speed of light in all matter. Who do you think that is?

We still don't hear about this because the energy that is present in everything that exists isn't fully explainable by science. Scientists strive to explain all things logically and all things must remain consistent in their world.

My desire through this book is to take the invisible world of what goes on in our minds and paint it through words so you can see it like the Word has told us to see it all along. To reveal what science has already uncovered as fact shows how incredible a created being you are. Every man and woman was created by God to create. We have no idea how creative we are every day. Chiefly, what a man thinks, he becomes. We can't see, touch, feel, or smell our thinking—it's invisible, but powerful.

Most of us don't gain enough knowledge or even have a clue about our hidden talents. Abilities we possess to heal ourselves, to do things we love, or to invent something no one has ever seen. These are only the beginning of the unlimited potential that lies within us.

Let's uncover the well of deep waters to your heart and tap into the living water within.

Chapter 2

Invisible Thoughts Grow Trees

I want to take you into the world of your invisible thoughts. How many of you know that your thoughts take up mental, residential real estate inside you? I mean this literally. Your brain actually shows this in ways that can be seen. Inside your brain, thoughts look like trees. (See figure 1.)

Figure 1: The brain from the top view, with dendrites, axons, and neurons.

Each neuron is a thought, with dendrite branch- like extensions where memories are stored. (See figure 2.)

Think Well, Live Well Now

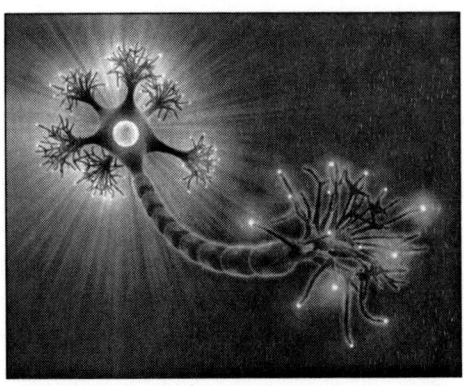

Figure 2: A Neuron (a thought) with an axon (stem) and dendrites (branches at the top).

Dr. Caroline Leaf in her book, *Who Switched Off My Brain?*, beautifully and simply explains how the wiring of the brain looks and performs like trees, with branches and fruit. (See figure 3.) In science they are called "The magic trees of the mind" because the nerve cells in the brain look like trees. Your brain is made up of all these trees or neurons that look like trees. We have forests in our brain. This blew me away to think about what the Bible says about trees and how they grow.

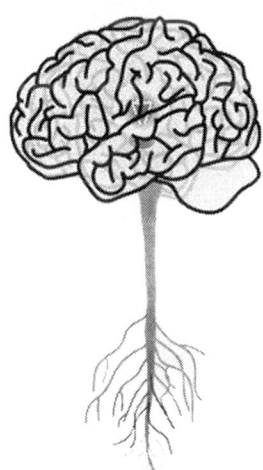

Figure 3: The brain full of dendrite branches with the brain stem (spinal cord) as the trunk.

If the thoughts are good, your trees flourish and grow to be mighty oaks, (see Figure 4.) If your thoughts are negative, you have a forest that looks like a fire went through it—or a tornado. (See figure 5.) Negative thoughts literally produce toxic, poisonous chemicals (hormones), which travel to all other cells throughout your body. Your body was so wonderfully designed to pass along electrical charges and chemicals; no system compares to it. The rate of flow and how quickly things happen is nothing short of amazing. With every thought there is a literal change that occurs in your brain and throughout the cells within your body. These changes are for good or bad, depending upon the type of thoughts you spend time dwelling on. You could think of your mind as a forest. You know how the wind blows in the forest in many ways? This is the comparison with thoughts and how they move through the forest in your brain.

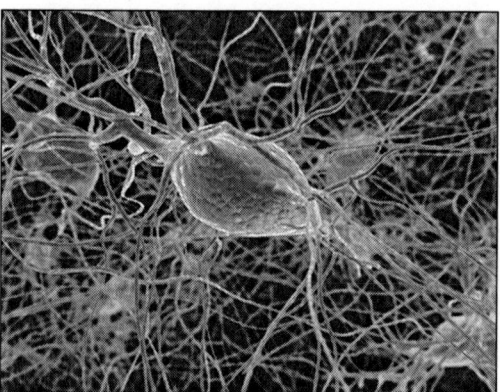

Figure 4: A representation of many branches of the brain of healthy thought.

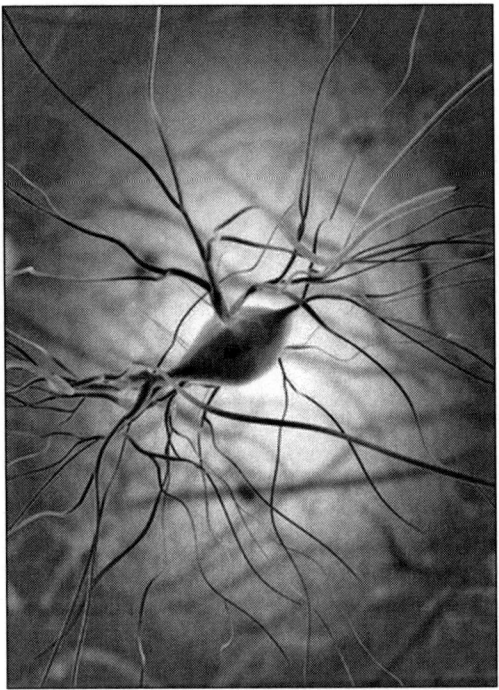

Figure 5: A representation of negative toxic thoughts.

You can have gentle breezes, strong winds, or tornado strength winds that move through your mind. Those and everything in between them will cause some sort of growing or changing of the forest landscape. Poisonous thoughts are like strong winds, up to tornado strength, and do damage just like they do in the earth. Thoughts that are good and full of life, make these trees of the mind grow big and strong, like mighty oaks.

Poisonous thoughts are toxic to your brain and other cells in your body. Dr. Leaf sights that researchers say that up to eighty seven percent of physical and mental health problems are a result of our thought lives. The reason you haven't heard about toxic thinking doing such damage is because it used to be thought that our brains were hard- wired with a fixed purpose and that they wear out. It was believed that our fate was predetermined by our genes and we have no choice; we are stuck with whatever we got from our parents.

The uncovered truth is that not one of us is bound to being a victim of our biology. You have an amazing, fantastic mind filled with any possibilities you want to engage it for. "All things are possible to those who believe," is true. The other amazing thing is you can turn things around for yourself at any age.

Why are thoughts so important, because they will shape your "trees." You can scan the brain of a drug addict and see how the landscape of trees looks sparse and burnt out. This is actually being done at the Amen Clinics by Dr. Daniel G. Amen, clinical neuroscientist, psychiatrist and brain-imaging specialist.

Your trees and the landscape of your brain can determine everything you become or don't become in life. The process of thinking will move thoughts through the same process, whether the thoughts are positive or negative. Every thought literally changes your brain and your body for life. This is why the Bible says, "As a man thinketh so is he." Scientists have shown that your thoughts cause changes down to the genetic level, literally restructuring cells in your body. This means that the thoughts you spend time thinking about literally multiply and grow and become living material in your brain, all under the radar of your five senses, or invisible to you. When these cells get restructured in a toxic form, scientists have seen how diseases form in our bodies.

Dr. Leaf, with twenty plus years of studying the brain, teaches the following about our brains and our thoughts. Emotions are triggered by thoughts. You have no emotions without thoughts producing them by the act of thinking. Thoughts produce biochemicals and electrical impulses that can flood the body with peace and balance or cause the body to go into stress. Stress is toxic thinking, plain and simple. Thoughts are chemicals, electrical impulses, and neurons living inside you. They look like trees with branches. The more good thoughts grow the more branches and trees form and connections become stronger. Negative thinking burns branches.

Depending upon what we change our thoughts to think into, some branches dissolve, new ones can form, and connections strengthen with good thoughts, or diminish from toxic thoughts. The brain holds an incredible ability to rewire itself at any age. This doesn't happen by fate (something that's unavoidable) or predestination (determined by someone else to be ours) or without our control. Each person controls every bit of this within their own brain. It all happens with thoughts and another person cannot climb in your brain and think for you. It happens under each person's own free will and their own total control. This is how each of us literally "creates" our own lives.

When you think, thoughts are active. This is why your brain isn't growing when you watch television or movies or video games in excess. Even doing the same thing over and over again can cause your imagination to become dormant from lack of use. A number of studies have been done that seem to indicate the more TV children watch, the lower their reading ability is.

As your brain thinks, thoughts create images. These photocopies are found in your cells and are what make up your memories. With each memory, there is an emotion attached to it. This is the process. These images are necessary for you to work with in order to imagine anything. Now think about what is allowed to be deposited into you as you engage in passive activity, such as TV. The eyes and ears are powerful gates for information downloads straight into our cells. We choose what kind of images we store in our long term memory by thoughts we dwell on and on what we allow our eyes and ears to take in.

Active thoughts activate attitudes. Attitudes come from our compiled thoughts and views. The more thoughts we have that are negative, the more our attitudes will match them. Attitudes are a reflection of internal images we have. They release chemicals into our cells that are carried throughout the entire body.

Chemicals: Signals Translating Information

Positive thoughts create positive attitudes because the correct amounts of chemicals get released into your system. Negative thoughts secrete distorted amounts of chemicals, disrupting the natural flow of hormones in your body. Chemicals are like little signals which translate the information of your thoughts into physical emotion. So thoughts, with emotions attached, produce attitudes. In turn, these produce a direct result in your body that is either positive or negative to your cellular balance. This is why you feel your emotions.

Once you feel an emotion, you can trace it back every time to what you were thinking at some point. Your thoughts are the keys to who you are, who you will become, and everything you will do. You have the total choice in every second of every day to choose what and how you think. "To paraphrase Deuteronomy 30:19b "Today you have the choice between life and death, blessings and curses."

When we are feeling out of balance or out of sorts, we have something negative going on in our thoughts. Positive thoughts create balance, while negative ones disrupt our body's balance. We are wired for positive operations only.

Healthy thoughts cause proper amounts and levels of chemicals to be released in us, building a strong foundation in the neural networks of our brains. Healthy, strong oak trees are what grow and multiply in our brain. The more positive thoughts you have, the larger the forest of the brain. And if you really want to build a strong foundation of mighty oak trees in your mind, you add the word of God to your thoughts. It is like putting your system on steroids (with a positive effect).

This is why the word of God is so important; it is living power. The results of that living power in the physically body are literally staggering. His word, when put in you as you meditate and think on it, brings unlimited potential for creation through you. The word of God is the only thing that can have a powerfully positive effect upon your operating system. It is living, breathing, and wants to take up residence in your heart and mind because of the extreme potential it can produce through you. It unpacks who you really could be. This is everyone's unseen treasure from God.

This is why the Bible says in Philippians 4:8, "Finally, brethren, whatsoever things are true, whatsoever things are honest, whatsoever things are just, whatsoever things are pure, whatsoever things are lovely, whatsoever things are of good report; if there be any virtue, and if there be any praise, think on these things." Hebrews 4:12 says, "For the word of God is quick, and powerful, and sharper than any two edged sword, piercing even to the dividing asunder of soul and spirit, and of the joints and marrow, and is a discerner of the thoughts and intents of the heart."

Stress is caused by Toxic Thought

Stress is caused by toxic thoughts. Improper amounts of endorphins and serotonin spew into our system by the direction of the mind-body connection. This connection is through the hypothalamus, pituitary, adrenal (HPA) command center. This is the system of your body that protects you from external threats. (The immune system protects you internally.) Your immune system kills cancer cells which are present in your body at all times. Don't gloss over that last sentence. Yes, cancer cells are already in your body. Cancer manifests from a strong enough breach to the immune system which causes a falling domino effect within the balances of the body.

The body was designed for growth, which is why God told man to multiply the earth. You can't multiply when you aren't growing something, right? The body is designed to be in either growth mode or protection mode. Your body needs to focus more on growing than on protecting itself. Your body automatically protects itself from the negative thoughts that spit distorted amounts of chemicals into your system. These toxic amounts of chemicals distort the DNA of the immune cells. The enemy always works to kill, steal and destroy us.

Our body was created with two systems to help communicate information to our trillions of cells; the nervous system and the hormone system. Both systems influence the immune system. The nervous system transmits rapidly between different body regions. The hormones are secretions produced by the command center, releasing chemicals through the bloodstream.

The hormone cortisol regulates and supports your heart, metabolism, and your immune system. Cortisol levels increase with stress. Remember, when you are stressed you are in protection mode and your body is working to survive. There is an excess amount of cortisol that flows through the brain and which causes your memories to shrink. It creates those burnt trees we talked about earlier. (see figure 6.) When the stress is removed, or when your mind isn't thinking of protecting the body any longer, the memories can come back. We can move into protection mode both non-consciously and consciously.

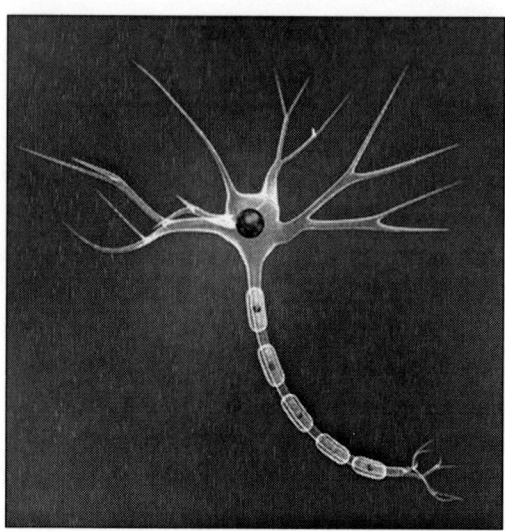

Figure 6: A burnt tree branch illustrated

We were created with a natural drug dispensary built into us. When we stay stressed the majority of the time, these toxic thoughts that cause your natural drug dispensary to keep spitting chemicals, can change the shape and destroy parts of the neurons. These negative changes go all the way down to your cellular level. Temporary stress can be managed by the body, but long term stress brings disease to the body.

Negative thoughts are fear based. The medical community knows this to be true. Dr. Caroline Leaf explained on Sid Roth's program "It's Supernatural" on September 27, 2010 that scientists say we are wired for love, and we learn fear. Fear is the hijack. When we are experiencing happiness, joy, peace, excitement there are chemicals that we secrete for each of those. Those chemicals in proper balance is what our physiology needs to operate in good health. That is why we are wired for love. Now when we experience the opposite of love such as fear, there is no known chemical in our body for the negative emotion of fear. So what the body does is take the chemical closest to that frequency distortion and secretes that chemical more and more, thus throwing the brain out of balance in its attempt to find the chemical for fear. This causes inflammation and imbalances. Fear triggers more than fourteen hundred known physical and chemical responses. This activates more than thirty different hormones and neurotransmitters, capable of throwing the body into a "frenzy."

In other words, the body gets overdosed with good chemicals. This causes inflammation in the brain. The brain takes a thought and translates it into a physical reaction inside our body through chemicals and nerve impulse. Inflammation then causes the immune system to break down. Thus 87% - 90% of all illnesses are a result of one's thought life. All thinking causes a physical structural change in the brain.

She explains that you have about a hundred billion nerve cells in your brain. Each nerve cell can grow up to two hundred thousand branches. That means we have about three hundred millions years worth of space in our brain to build memories. There could be more than that. The non-conscious mind is building memory constantly. Every single thing we hear and that comes in through our five senses converts when we think about it. Then we make choices and it converts into a structural thing in your brain, which is a thought and they look like trees. That is why the scientists refer to them as "The magic trees of the mind"

21 Days to Regrow New Trees

The good news is that we can rewire our trees in twenty-one days. We can change the way our genes express themselves. Yes, we control what our genes do. Genes make proteins, and proteins are the building blocks that build our thoughts. I will go into more detail about genes later on this book, but for now I will say that above our genes are epigenomes. Our thoughts are electrical and flow down to the gene level and those thoughts, plus those we have stored, will activate either a good or bad gene blueprint.

Our non-conscious mind is filled with trees with either negative black burnt branches, or flourishing green branches. Life circumstances and various stimuli activate different thoughts we have, which are stored memories. This causes these stored thoughts to move from your non-conscious mind, to your conscious mind. When thoughts move to your conscious mind, they become plastic and can be reformed. This is known as neuroplasticity.

The frontal lobe of our brain enables us to look at ourselves from the outside in, to look at these stored thoughts, and "take them captive" as the Word says we should do. If we say we "can't" change what the thought is telling us, that same thought moves back to our non-conscious mind and becomes more toxic. The more we keep moving the thought back to our non-conscious, the more toxic it becomes.

Because we are wired for love, we need chemicals generated by thoughts, words, and actions of love to flow around the tree to melt it down of toxic stored thought. Then we can build next to it the healthy tree. The thought can remain in our consciousness 24-48 hours before it returns to memory. During this time we can change it.

As you speak the word of God to the burnt trees in your mind, the more chemicals begin to flow to melt the toxic branches in the brain down. The combination of dopamine, oxytocin, serotonin and a few other chemicals, literally melt the negative thoughts. Then we can rebuild the healthy tree next to it. The mind is renewed. (The chemicals are what carry the physical pain, inflammation, etc.)

You can not have a green tree with a burnt tree in the same tree at the same time. (see figure 7 & 8.) There is a scripture in 1 John 4:18 that says perfect love expels fear. "There is no fear in love; but perfect love casteth out fear: because fear hath torment" That is what is literally happening on a scientific level in twenty-one days. As we look at what God has told us in His word about our physiology, we can see how science has proven the word of God to be true.

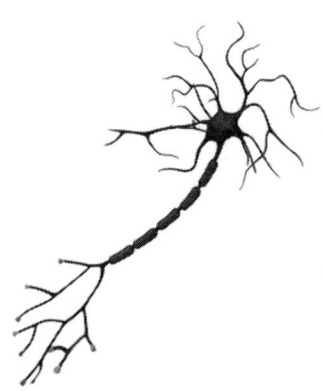 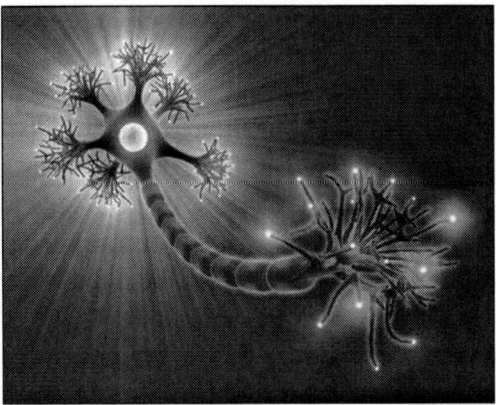

Figure 7: Burnt branches illustrated Figure 8: Green branches illustrated

Luke 21:26 warns of "Men's hearts failing them for fear." Men's hearts will fail them for fear (anxiety and worry). Proverbs 16:24 teaches us, "Pleasant words are as an honeycomb, sweet to the soul, and health to the bones." Pleasant words are health to our bones— they bring health to us. Do you know where the immune system is located in your body? You guessed it—in the bone marrow.

Thoughts of love, peace, joy, gentleness, caring, compassion, trusting, and laughter— all that are good and true, build a solid foundation in our immune system. Philippians 4:8 says, "Finally, brethren, whatsoever things are true, whatsoever things are honest, whatsoever things are just, whatsoever things are pure, whatsoever things are lovely, whatsoever things are of good report; if there be any virtue, and if there be any praise, think on these things." Replacing the word "things" with "thoughts," read the verse shown above, one more time.

Negative thoughts will allow stress to become engrafted into the trees of your mind. James 1:21 says, "receive with meekness the engrafted word, which is able to save your souls." When you purpose in your mind to do this, your immune system will be the defensive army that protects you from illness and disease, both in your body and in your mind. Toxic thoughts prevent this and begin to destroy your immune system.

Just as you think yourself into stress, your thoughts can also, without a doubt, wash away stress. Ephesians 5:26 says, "That he might sanctify and cleanse it with the washing of water by the word." Holding our thoughts captive before just letting them fly on through our system is the key. Second Corinthians 10:5 expresses this more fully: "Casting down imaginations, and every high thing that exalteth itself against the knowledge of God, and bringing into captivity every thought to the obedience of Christ."

Most of us walk around with the idea that we are doomed to repeat behavior and life patterns of our family members—our biology controls us and we cannot rise above the influences of our environment. We have been deceived. We can detoxify our thoughts, and when we do, we reform those branches (pathways) within four days and make new ones in twenty days.

This is where misconceptions about positive thinking come into play. It isn't just about reciting positive affirmations. You can do that all day long and it still will not change anything for you. You must take a toxic thought back, hold it captive, and put it back through a rebuilding sequence. The old form of it must be reformed into something new.

If you are getting the idea that the difference is made in our lives by how we choose to think about and respond to whatever we experience, you are correct. If we learn to cope properly, and deal with our thoughts correctly, we will determine a positive outcome for our lives. If you control and trash incoming information before it is hard wired into your brain, you can positively affect who you are. We always have the ability to rewire our brain. Proverbs 23:7 says, "For as he thinketh in his heart, so is he." What we see is what we say and is what we become.

Chapter 3

How Thoughts Are Processed Physiologically

All information we receive enters through one of our five senses. Information we receive is processed far more than we think. It is processed through the thalamus, similarly to how an air traffic controller controls the planes that fly in a certain section of sky. This processing by the thalamus allows the brain to receive large amounts of data from the external and internal world all at once. The thalamus transmits electrical data that activates existing thoughts (nerve cells) in the outer part of the brain called the cerebral cortex.

The nerve cells in the cerebral cortex look like trees. Information being processed creates a "wind" blowing through the trees. This wind activates all thoughts on the trees, and the result of this is your attitude. Your attitude is an expression of your emotions. Your attitude will always be activated, no matter how much you try to keep it hidden. Your attitude is then transmitted from the thalamus down to the hypothalamus.

The hypothalamus regulates the chemicals from your natural "drug dispensary." You could say that it prepares a response to your thoughts. No wonder it is referred to as the "brain" of the endocrine system. The endocrine system is a collection of glands and organs which produce and regulate your hormones. It spews hormones that are needed to deal with perceived threats to your system. It affects your emotional functions.

Let's say you worry a lot. This is the process that is going on inside of you when you worry. The hypothalamus will respond by spitting massive amounts of chemical imbalances to the pituitary gland (master gland of the endocrine system). Your worries put your operating system in protection mode, which restricts you from thinking clearly, making wise decisions, or developing healthy thoughts.

If you change your attitude from a negative one to a positive one, the hypothalamus will release a balance of chemicals that produce the feeling of peace. Then the rest of your system will spew the correct ingredients of neurotransmitters for good thought building. If it sounds like you are a building contractor, you are correct.

To help with making good choices, we were given the amygdala and hippocampus. The amygdala deals with passionate, perceptual emotions being attached to incoming thoughts. It is the library that looks to match some stored memory with incoming thoughts. The amygdala handles both positive and negative emotions. It is like a library for emotional perceptions that occur each time thought is built. Every time we build a memory, we activate emotions. Emotions are what give the "bling" to thoughts. ("Bling" is slang for "flashy, glitzy.")

The amygdala communicates with the hypothalamus like two female teenagers on the phone— all the time. The amygdala has communication to the frontal lobe, where reasoning, decision-making, analyzing and strategizing occurs. This is important because this is where emotions are balanced to insure proper reactions. This point is critical to your health and well-being. If you choose to stop thinking about the negative thoughts, they will disappear. This happens immediately upon your direction. When you choose not to think about them, they fade away.

If you don't stop thinking about them and continue to focus on them, they flow to the hippocampus. The hippocampus deals with memory and motivation. The hippocampus is where the importance you attach to thoughts is filed, both short term and long term memories. This is where thoughts become permanent and become who you are. Most of this happens as you sleep.

The hippocampus is very susceptible to chemical hormones from stress. Stress can cause the hippocampus to lose cells and shrink. There are tiny openings on cells that are receptors of chemical information from your thoughts. Lack of communication between the hippocampus and the central house of the brain causes one to be unable to make good memories.

No Thought is Harmless

No thought should be allowed to control you. No thought is harmless. Your thoughts are an electrical light show creating or destroying branches of information. Existing memories and current thoughts move around like an electrical light show from the hippocampus up to the front part of the brain (basal forebrain, located just behind the inside corners of your eyes). This information is amplified each time it moves to the front of your brain.

The hippocampus holds thoughts and memories for 24 to 48 hours. This spectacular event is decision in motion. When these thoughts are being amplified here, they are very unstable, which means they are changeable. But they must be either changed altogether, or they will be reinforced, making them even stronger. The harder we think on those thoughts and memories, the more change we make. The change will be greater reinforcement of the old memory or a total change of what it was. This process is called protein synthesis.

Science has found that we can make the choice to interfere with protein synthesis by engaging new thoughts. So if you want to change old bad memories into good ones, you must do it consciously. It won't happen non-consciously. This is what the Bible refers to as renewing your mind. Romans 12:2 says, "And be not conformed to this world: but be ye transformed by the renewing of your mind, that ye may prove what is that good, and acceptable, and perfect, will of God." How is this done? Second Corinthians 10:5b says, "bringing into captivity every thought to the obedience of Christ."

When you bring your thoughts captive, the actual physical structure of the brain changes. This process is called neuroplasticity. Thinking causes neurotransmitters, which are chemicals in the brain that carry electrical impulses, to flow. "Neuro" refers to neuron connections. "Plasticity" refers to the growth of those neurons and connections. As we learn something, we increase plasticity into our being. We create more and more connections. We grow branches on our trees. The more we do this, the more connections we grow.

Consider the emotion of fear as an example. Over time, we make connections of fear with people, our job, driving—any number of things. When we do this, we develop many connections to fear. Neuron connections want to stay alive and need only three things to do so: oxygen, sugar and stimulation. Keep in mind, thoughts are stimulation.

To change a long-term memory of fear, a pre-programmed fear in our memory, we must focus reprogramming that fear with a higher thought. The thoughts must be rewritten according to a higher sense of knowledge. The higher knowledge comes from learning how to change your self-talk—what you say about yourself in your head. This is accomplished by storing words in your head that are positive, loving, trusting, and that speak of who you are in God. The word of God is your beginning source of knowledge.

In this way, you actually begin to grow a new pathway, different from the old which would have taken you down a destructive pathway and straight into panic. You don't beat yourself up. This is critical to establish early on in your understanding. This is a big deal because new green branches grow and multiply only when you use positive words in your head? The longer you spend kicking yourself for slipping up in the moment, there is no new growth of good branches but rather more ashes being formed from burning or reinforcing the same old burnt thoughts.

You must remember to tell yourself that you are walking in the grace of God and that He protects you—it will work out. When you do this, you actually begin to grow new pathways because of neuroplasticity that says, "He has made me safe, and will protect me. He will work this out and all will be okay."

The old pathways dissolve over time because if you don't use them, you lose them. In the proteins that develop, in the process called protein synthesis, if you have a hundred proteins, you will lose fifty of them in fourteen days. And in another fourteen days you will lose twenty-five more. So in twenty-eight days those cells are beginning to degenerate and we are only left with one quarter of the original number of living cells. This is where the twenty-eight days to break any habit comes from. Not allowing stimulation of these old thoughts prevents neurons from keeping the old pathway alive. This emphasizes again the importance of using positive words and positive self-talk in your mind because any negativity just stimulates the old neural pathways to go deeper. You kill them or grow them with your thoughts.

Your mind needs to be renewed with truth, real truth, which is only found in the word of God. The Word is the instruction manual for how man was created to operate. Would you try to fix a Mercedes using a repair manual for a Chevy? Of course not! Only the truth of the word of God can repair or renew the mind.

As your mind is renewed, your old thoughts are dying and going away. Transneuronal degeneration means that the neuron wants to stay alive, but it is dying. As it gets weaker and weaker, it begins to fire on its own. So now you need to understand that you have been walking in who you were created to be and these neurons are losing their power and effect to suddenly start firing at random. You are up against the wall and wonder what is going on—you were doing so well. This is when you must push against those dying thoughts with your new thoughts. The moment you allow yourself to think on the old thoughts is the moment when you give them permission to regrow.

Have you ever been moving along and doing well, when suddenly you are overwhelmed with fearful thoughts, like a rushing river? Don't let the river flow. People perish for their lack of knowledge of this. Don't be ignorant. This is the physiological process your mind undergoes when it is being renewed by the washing of the word.

Over our lifetime, most of us develop multiple pathways of fear, possibly hundreds. As our mind is renewed maybe hundred pathways can be closed, but we should not be surprised when old fears show up, stimulated by any number of experiences. Just do what you know to do and deal with these the same way you dealt with the other hundreds of. Don't take the bait to have fear.

You may have developed a fear of snakes when you were told as a child that they are poisonous and that their bite could put you in the hospital. So one weekend, you decide to go camping, something you had not done previously. You are sitting around a campfire, when along comes a snake. The camping trip triggers the fear of the snake but you didn't know to deal with that fear until the snake showed up and exposed the fear. No matter how old the memory of fear is, each fear must be dealt with as events expose the need to change the pathway. You need to deal with it by renewing your mind the same way you did with the other fears. This neurological pathway will be put to death by the renewing of your mind, just like the others. Deal with the fear in each experience as it comes. This is the true process of renewing your mind.

Our brains were wonderfully created by God. The more mental practice of positive imagination and reflection on what you really want that is good, the stronger and healthier the trees in your brain will be at any age. The power of your mind can do so much more than you probably ever imagined.

In Genesis 11 there is a story that illustrates the power of our thoughts. The people saw in their minds a tower to build. They thought to themselves that they could build the tower all the way to heaven. God had to stop them by causing confusion and making it impossible for them to communicate, for the tower had become an idol to them. The word says, "Nothing they have imagined they can do will be impossible for them" (Genesis 11:6, AMP). God had to stop them. Can you imagine? We all can.

Mentally rehearsing things on a daily basis is how we change what is stored in our memories from bad to good. (It works the other way also!) Healthy thoughts or toxic thoughts, whichever we rehearse the most, will be built into our minds. We choose to tear down strongholds, say of fear, by bringing it into conscious awareness and reforming it with new thought. We must replace it with healthy information, as in Philippians 4:8, "Finally, brethren, whatsoever things are true, whatsoever things are honest, whatsoever things are just, whatsoever things are pure, whatsoever things are lovely, whatsoever things are of good report; if there be any virtue, and if there be any praise, think on these things."

Keep thy Heart with all Diligence

Your heart is the checkpoint for all emotions. The emotions come to it by the flow of chemicals your thoughts have sent. Your heart checks in with your brain to verify the accuracy and integrity of your thoughts. Too many people do not pay attention to this step. They get used to overlooking what their heart is telling them, to the point where their heart becomes hard. We could consider this as a possible meaning for the word of God speaking about the heart becoming hardened. In the cases of open heart surgery it is seen how the heart has formed scar tissue, causing it to become hardened and less pliable to pump blood.

With every decision you make, which includes what you say back to someone in conversations, a quiet word of advice will come to you from your heart. If you listen to what your heart tells you, it secretes the ANF (atrial natriuretic factor) hormone which gives you a feeling of peace. If you don't listen to your heart, you won't feel peace. Proverbs 4:23 says, "Keep thy heart with all diligence; for out of it are the issues of life."

We were designed to think deeply and to meditate on healthy thoughts because we were wired for love. Protein synthesis makes your thoughts a part of you by repetition and by rehearsing them in frequent intervals. This repetition is necessary and is always happening with toxic or non-toxic thought. For this reason, if you want to make changes to your memories, you must think on those changes more than one time. This is why scripture tells us to meditate on the Word so it causes a renewing of your mind. Romans 12:2 says; "be ye transformed by the *renewing of your mind*, that ye may prove what is good."

John 15:5 says, "I am the vine, ye are the branches: He that abideth in me, and I in him, the same bringeth forth much fruit: for without me ye can do nothing." You bear fruit when you become who God designed you to be. The only way you will bear much fruit is by understanding that controlling your thoughts is absolutely essential. They cause you to be electrically wired for health or disease; becoming who you were designed to be or someone that is toxic to yourself and those around you.

You are the Architect and Contractor

This is what is dynamic about our thought life. Most people feel powerless and helpless when it comes to trying to change who they are. Why? Because they falsely believe that they have no control over certain "genetic" aspects of themselves. Most have been incorrectly taught, "You are the way you are because it is in your genes." Not so!

The power of your thoughts is much stronger than you ever imagined. By thinking, you exercise your free will and make choices. Those choices access which genes are utilized in your nerve cells. This process is called epigenetics. Our genes hold many different possible blueprints. Our thoughts and decisions express any number of blueprints, all of which are housed in our nerve cells. You are the architect and contractor of how you build your life. Proverbs 23:7 says, "For as he thinks in his heart, so is he" is a literal fact.

To summarize this: your cells have blueprints in the genes, but not all of them are accessed at one time. When a blueprint is accessed, it makes a new protein which alters its structure and functional capabilities. Just as a building is constructed according to a blueprint to look a certain way; that is what it will look like to the public. The ingredients of how to make these proteins is read by the individual gene. Therefore, it is the thought and choice of our free will that determines which blueprints are utilized or activated. The truth is we have control over the genes that shape us—our thinking. Our behavior follows our thoughts. This is the house we build and put on display for everyone to see.

This is exciting because we can change our building to look like something different at any time, or at any age. But this is a process that doesn't happen overnight, without effort and action—taking our thoughts captive. We are not victims of our biology (or our parents). Taking our thoughts captive is the key to rebuilding behaviors that are negative or harmful. It is also the key to getting and keeping us healthy and successful, while prospering in our talents.

It isn't just our brain that stores memories; the cells throughout our body store memory. In biofeedback therapy, it is possible to tell whether a person has experienced certain illnesses because of stored memory in cells. The communication takes place between the cells in your body and the brain.

For example, your brain takes information from your thoughts and interprets them as fear or anxiety. Then every immune cell gets that interpretation instantly. This is known as the mind-body connection, identified earlier as your hypothalamus-pituitary-adrenal (HPA) command center. There are two primary emotions: fear and love. All other emotions are branches from the root of either love or fear.

Each of these causes its own physiological effects. Emotions affect our anatomy because of the balance or lack of balance in the amount of chemicals (cortisol, dopamine, serotonin, etc) that get released into the body. If you make a habit of suppressing, ignoring, or trying to deny your emotions, you disrupt your internal network flow, which causes disorder to peptide flow and the connections to your reactions. This is toxic to emotions and to your proper thinking and decision making.

What I expound on next will connect more dots comprehending what happens in the human thought process.

Thoughts are Invisible Energy in Motion

Everything seen is moving energy. Everything vibrates at its own unique frequency or set of frequencies. Thoughts are invisible energy in motion. All matter is made up of atoms. Atoms are frequencies of energy. Atoms have different energy, frequencies, and vibrations. Thoughts too hold different energy, with different vibrations. Thoughts can be measured; they have weight. They also affect other energy and vibrations they come into contact with, both internally and externally.

Some things vibrate higher than others. The higher the vibration of energy, the more refined the light. Higher vibrational energy is capable of creating new things. God is the ultimate light. Some things vibrate at a lower, denser rate as they are slower or heavier; they have less light. Low vibrations tear things apart and destroy things.

Examples of high vibrational thoughts would be: love, forgiveness, peace, honor, integrity, joy, rest, discernment, wisdom, compassion, mercy, nature, respect, orderliness, laughter, health, good relationships, and more.

Examples of low vibrational thoughts would be: fear, anger, hatred, lust, dishonor, jealousy, envy, gossip, hurt, greed, guilt, accusation, bitterness, unforgiveness, deceit, despair, depression, suicide, addictions, pride, ego, improper speech, lies, and more.

Notice the many emotions listed above as either high or low vibrational thoughts. The highest emotion with the strongest amount of light and power is love. The ultimate of all energies, emotions, and vibrational quality is love. Mark 12:30 says, "And thou shalt love the Lord thy God with all thy heart, and with all thy soul, and with all thy mind, and with all thy strength: this is the first commandment. And the second is like, namely this, Thou shalt love thy neighbor as thyself. There is none other commandment greater than these."

The emotion with the strongest amount of darkness is probably fear. Fear is mentioned over five hundred times in the Bible. Hate is an emotion that develops from fear. Therefore fear holds more power in darkness. You can't love when you fear. First John 4:18 says (my notes in parentheses), "There is no fear in love; (because they are different frequencies) but perfect love casteth out fear (because love is light and is the strongest frequency): because fear hath torment. He that feareth is not made perfect in love." Second Timothy 1:7, "For God hath not given us the spirit of fear; but of power, and of love, and of a sound mind." God can't give us negative energy of any nature because that energy isn't found in Him.

The Positive and Negative Control System

I will paint a picture for you. Imagine an invisible horizon inside of us, where our thoughts rise above or fall below. Higher vibrational thoughts are above the horizon and bring more light and life into our bodies, and they exude from our bodies. Lower vibrational thoughts take us below the horizon of light, into darkness, tearing down or bringing decay and destruction to our physiology. We also affect others with our energetic thoughts for good or bad because we transmit and receive energy from everything and everyone around us. The object is to keep your thoughts above the horizon, to capture more light which is needed to grow healthy green trees.

Understand that when you engage positive thoughts from above the horizon of light, you also engage or activate your positive control system. When you activate negative dark thoughts from below the horizon, you are activating your negative control system. You are the one who activates the switches. You have the power to choose which system you activate, the positive control system or the negative control system.

Emotions are not neutral. They carry a charge of energy that is either positive or negative. Positive controlling emotions have the energetic power to create and cause harmony, and form a union with the Kingdom of God. Negative controlling emotions have the power to destroy us, both inside and out. Both systems cannot operate at the same time, but they can shift back and forth quickly. Remember that the Bible says you can't serve two masters. You will love the one and hate the other. Matthew 6:24, "No man can serve two masters: for either he will hate the one, and love the other; or else he will hold to the one, and despise the other."

Emotions carry a nature to them. The emotion of love has a love nature, just as the emotion of fear has a fear nature. Emotions are formed from a thought that had a feeling. We took that feeling and gave it more energy by thinking about it or dwelling on it. Those feelings became stronger until they formed a stored emotional memory within us. Emotions are strong feelings. When the nature of the emotion "expresses" itself, we call that expression an attitude. Attitudes are an emotion, expressing its nature.

So the emotions or natures that fall below the horizon are the ones that have an emphasis upon self, the big "I," our ego. The emotional natures that rise above the horizon cause the heart to be congruent with our mind, in turn causing our operating system to be in harmony for good health and well-being. Think of the expression of feeling light hearted. When we focus our thinking more on the emotions and thoughts of the light, we stay more heart-centered.

The word heart is mentioned almost nine hundred times in the Word. Proverbs 14:30 says, "A sound heart is the life of the flesh: but envy the rottenness of the bones." It is plain to see how our physiology needs the higher vibrations of light to sustain life and health in us.

You are more single-minded the majority of your thoughts and emotional memories are above your horizon, because they come with a nature full of light. Your physiology and spirit become unstable when you stay divided between the natures (emotion) from both below and above your horizon.

James 1:8, "A double minded man is unstable in all his ways." Later in the chapter on the heart you will discover that the heart also has thought. You can become double-minded when your heart thinks one way and your mind thinks the opposite for too long. It has to do with how you control your thinking both in your heart and your mind. You are either more full of light (life) or more full of darkness (death). This affects your body.

Thinking thoughts and holding on to emotional memories from below the horizon dims the very essence of who you are, and draws you into darkness or below the horizon. You are either more full of light and energy, or you have less energy and feel drained. Thinking more thoughts from below the horizon never will give you enough power to get above the horizon. That would be like saying you can fill yourself with more darkness to gain light; it is impossible.

The negative operating system of natures found below the horizon is powerless to create any new life and harmony within you, rather they will destroy the harmony and any good feelings you have about yourself. They have no power other than to steal light from you. However, the opposite of this is true with positive thoughts and emotions above the horizon.

Activating your positive controls is like giving yourself light and energy in the middle of a power outage—they have the light of life to create. That operating system can dispel the energy from dark memories of the past and change thoughts to create necessary energy for you. High frequencies of light are able to create unlimited new possibilities. It is the glory light of God that heals wounds from negative spoken words. You cancel negative words by speaking out to cancel them. Until then, they are still out there in the atmosphere.

Like energy attracts like energy. It is important to be careful of those with whom you have relationships. If someone thrives on emotional natures from below the horizon, it will be necessary for them to stay there to get their energy. It requires a renewing of the mind for them to even realize that they are settling for the weakest of energy in their systems. This is why it is such a never-ending spiral for so many people, going lower and lower. They don't understand that they are transmitting and receiving energy and that the longer they stay below the horizon with those thoughts of emotion, the less they will want to go the other direction, toward the light. The longer those energies are transmitting and receiving, the easier it is for those emotions to multiply in strength. They will literally feel less and less light energy and increasingly powerless to receive the light.

Practice more Unforgiveness, get more Negative Energy.

Someone who thinks thoughts of anger, bitterness, and jealousy will need more of those thoughts to keep giving them energy to exist. In a twisted way they feel as if they become stronger when they can attract more negative energy to them. These people will gravitate toward other negative people or try to pull the light out of others with their negative words. You need more darkness to sustain energy than you do light. Unforgiveness and bitterness are duo thought, the ultimate drain of energy. The person who lives in that thinking will need more of that energy to keep going, so naturally they will practice more unforgiveness to get more energy. This is why holding unforgiveness within us damages us more than the person toward whom we hold unforgiveness.

The unblocking energy within you is forgiveness. This is why God told us to forgive seventy times seven, that is, every time. Matthew 18:21-22 says, "Then came Peter to him, and said, Lord, how oft shall my brother sin against me, and I forgive him? till seven times? Jesus saith unto him, I say not unto thee, Until seven times: but, Until seventy times seven." This thought energy is dangerous to our health, both physically and mentally.

This is why it is so important to consider what our Creator God told us to do. Matthew 6:15 says, "But if you do not forgive others their trespasses [their reckless and willful sins, leaving them, letting them go, and giving up resentment], neither will your Father forgive you your trespasses" (AMP). The beneficiary of forgiveness is the one who forgives, not the forgiven one. Emotions above the horizon are literally uplifting.

I used to think that my thoughts were my own private things. After all, no one can read my mind, nor can they know what I am thinking. This may be true, but that doesn't mean that your thoughts aren't harmful, both to yourself and to others. Do we let our thoughts go off and do their own thing, or do we direct them? Who is responsible for what we think if no other human can get into our head?

What company do we keep in our minds? What do those friendships of our mind produce, both in us and by what we speak and receive from others? Do we allow our thoughts to be reckless or disciplined? Are you directing good or bad energy, or recklessly allowing energy to fly around at random? It is totally in your control but must be managed by none other than you.

The same is true for the words we speak. Our thoughts come from our heart and our lives are created by our thoughts and what we speak. Our words are energy that either heal or destroy our lives, as well as the lives of others. I used to ignorantly believe that words made no difference and had no power. I knew that the word of God said, "Death and life are in the power of the tongue, and they who indulge in it shall eat the fruit of it [for death or life]" (Proverbs 18:21, AMP). But like many, I still didn't give it enough credit. There is energetic power in what we speak which comes from what our thoughts have been building.

Healing comes by what we speak. Proverbs 12:18 says, "There are those who speak rashly, like the piercing of a sword, but the tongue of the wise brings healing" (AMP). While Proverbs 15:4 says, "A gentle tongue [with its healing power] is a tree of life" (AMP). Did you notice it says tree?

Remember, we learned that power is greater in the thought/emotional energy from above the horizon. Love holds the greatest energy. Those higher frequencies are the emotions of energy that create. They are full of light and life. The lower frequencies from thoughts/emotions below the horizon only destroy and tear down things. They are full of darkness, death, and destruction.

Now think about what you speak. Which words do you use day in and day out? Consider your life. Are you where you want to be? Do you live in perfect health, harmony, balance (homeostasis)? Are you struggling with disease and sickness? Our thoughts and words hold intentions from our heart.

Luke 6:45, "A good man out of the good treasure of his heart bringeth forth that which is good; and an evil man out of the evil treasure of his heart bringeth forth that which is evil: for of the abundance of the heart his mouth speaketh." Our tongue will speak what is in our heart because it is the root system of our thoughts. It reveals it for others to know. It bears our fruit for others to see, which comes from the fruit of the trees in our brain. What you see you say and become.

The body seeks homeostasis (balance) all the time by coordinating mental processes with biology to cause good behavior and health. Keeping this flow is the key for controlling negative, toxic thoughts. If our emotions are blocked for long periods of time, we won't feel what we should feel. Through neuroplasticity, we have built a rut that tells us we are not allowed to feel. It creates logjams in the brain that stop thinking processes from flowing properly.

At this point, it would be good to step back to what happens to develop "trees" in our brain. Thought is required to create an emotion. So where do thoughts come from? One of three places: the Kingdom of God, the kingdom of sin (the devil's kingdom) or, our own stored memories. How can we tell where our thoughts are coming from? We cannot know, unless we hold our thoughts captive. There are many winds (thoughts) that blow in our mind every nanosecond. This is the invisible world of the Spirit that the Bible talks about.

There is outside interference, static on our lines, which blows through our thoughts. Thoughts resulting in the emotions from above the horizon come from the Kingdom of God. Emotions from below the horizon come from the kingdom of sin. Our own thoughts are generated from current events, triggering current new thoughts in us, coupled with thoughts in long-term memory.

We are responsible to grow good thoughts, to add good strong branches to our trees. This can only be accomplished with thoughts that come from above the horizon, from light, which produce chemicals in proper balance which are released into the system, producing good fruit. The trees of your brain can only produce good branches and good fruit by abiding in the vine. John 15:5 says, "I am the vine, ye are the branches: He that abideth in me, and I in him, the same bringeth forth much fruit: for without me ye can do nothing." Little do many of us realize how literal God can be in what He tells us in His word.

This means that we must experience emotions of caring, compassion, appreciation, gratefulness, hopefulness, peacefulness, trust, laughter, and the most powerful energy of all, love. These emotions produce value in your body and soul, creating health. The issues of the heart, mind, will, and emotions are absolutely critical.

Chapter 4

The Heart has Intelligence

There is not only a brain in our head, but in our heart as well. At the institute of HeartMath, in Boulder Creek, California researchers have confirmed what our intuition and the word of God have told us: The heart is the interconnection of communication and interaction between consciousness and the physiological responses that generate emotions.

Studies have shown that the coherency, with which the heart leads our system, creates more intelligence within us and reduces the activity of the sympathetic nervous system, which is responsible for our fight or flight instinct. While it does that, it also increases growth the parasympathetic nervous system handles. When we willfully activate our positive control system of feelings like love, gratitude, and care, it causes physiological responses which provide longer, healthier lives. You read that right; our heart gives us longer life because we remain healthier.

Yes, our heart has a brain and has thoughts. Scripture tells us this. Imagination takes place in the heart. This is important to remember because we are going to take a look at how and what the sin kingdom does to our hearts to try and prevent this. Your enemy is really after your heart. We are going to increasing understand why? Acts 5:3 says, "But Peter said, Ananias, why has Satan filled your heart that you should lie to and attempt to deceive the Holy Spirit?" (AMP)

It is important to understand why and how this happens to us. Here is one clue from 2 Corinthians 1:22: "[He has also appropriated and acknowledged us as His by] putting His seal upon us and giving us His [Holy] Spirit in our hearts as the security deposit and guarantee [of the fulfillment of His promise].

Everything God does is with seed. There is a period of time for that seed to grow and show fruit for harvesting. He is all about seed time and harvest. All of His creation has seed to reproduce for multiplication. God told Adam and Eve to multiply and replenish the earth but that means more than just having babies. When you were created in the mind of God, even before you were conceived, He put seeds within you. These seeds are the purposes He created you alone to accomplish.

With our heart we form beliefs. To believe is to have confidence in the truth of, existence of, or reliability of something—without absolute proof that one is right in doing so. To perceive is to recognize, discern, envision, or understand; to become aware of, know, or identify by means of the senses.

To affect your heart, the enemy has to corrupt the seeds that God put within you for what you have the potential to become. He then comes along to change any positive beliefs you have into his negative beliefs—he strives to program his belief systems into you. He is working to alter your perception.

How you perceive something comes from what you believe to be true about it. Our perceptions can exist without absolute proof that they are right to believe. Your beliefs are things that you have confidently established within yourself to be the truth, to have existence, or to be reliable—without absolute proof that you are right for believing it. This is how he attempts to program you to see things like he sees them. He started at conception, before you were born, and does not stop until you are dead. His kingdom works hard to cause you to perceive things the way he needs you to perceive them, using your five senses. Our five senses only allow us to perceive from the "outside in."

God doesn't want us to perceive with only five senses. He teaches us to perceive, through the Holy Spirit with our spirit, which goes beyond the capability of what the five physical senses perceive. He wants us to exercise our spirits to perceive from the inside out. This is why the kingdom of God is on the inside of you. We were created to perceive from the inside out, not the outside in. This is why our heart is vital to our operations. (We will cover more about perception after exploring the heart in more physiological detail.)

Our enemy doesn't want us to have our godly spiritual senses active. Why, because those senses make us more aware of his deceptions. With the Holy Spirit inside of us, the seeds planted inside our hearts grow us into our purpose and destiny. This is not good news for Satan, that is, to have the Kingdom of God grow and multiply. So he tries to keep us in our heads, limited to the logic of what can be believed through only the five physical senses. By planting thoughts he gives us, he goes straight for the heart to harden it, changing as much truth from God as he can into a lie. Second Thessalonians 2:13 says, ".... because God hath from the beginning chosen you to salvation through sanctification of the Spirit and belief of the truth."

He knows we will find God's truth when we use our hearts. Jeremiah 29:13 says, "And ye shall seek me, and find me, when ye shall search for me with all your heart." But that is only the beginning of what you carry that the enemy is after. Before exploring that, notice some verses that talk about the heart:

Luke 5:22: "But when Jesus perceived their thoughts, he answering said unto them, What reason ye in your hearts?"

Mark 2:8: "And immediately when Jesus perceived in his spirit that they so reasoned within themselves, he said unto them, Why reason ye these things in your hearts?"

Mark 8:17: "And when Jesus knew it, he saith unto them, Why reason ye, because ye have no bread? perceive ye not yet, neither understand? have ye your heart yet hardened?"

There is a literal hardening of the heart that happens the more the heart develops scar tissue. Remember, your spirit and the Holy Spirit resides in the throne room of your heart, resonating and growing outward from there. The enemy knows when you are resonating, or growing with the truth of the word of God because it has a rhythm, flow, frequency and energy contrary to the kingdom of sin. To Satan and others in his kingdom, that resonance and those frequencies are felt as "discord." We can't bluff them; we put off frequencies of energy. He can't read or hear our exact thoughts but he knows if they are vibrations in harmony with God by the discord they cause in his vibrations.

The heart contains seeds and is the root system, to grow branches in the brain, which bear fruit that come from the roots, which come from the seeds in you.

What happens to the root system affects the condition of the tree. The seeds we water and grow within us will determine what type of tree we become and what fruit we bear. When the seeds are planted in good ground, the root system is strong enough to support the whole tree, and the tree will bear much fruit. Multiplication is what God intended for man to do, to fill the earth with Himself. But if the seed isn't planted in fertile soil, the roots will be weak and shallow, and the branches will lack fruit.

Take a look at the illustration from an internal view of our body. It gives you a picture of how our heart is the ground for seeds to take root in. They grow up the trunk of our spinal column and into our head, where branches are developed with thoughts from the heart. (See figures 9 and 10.)

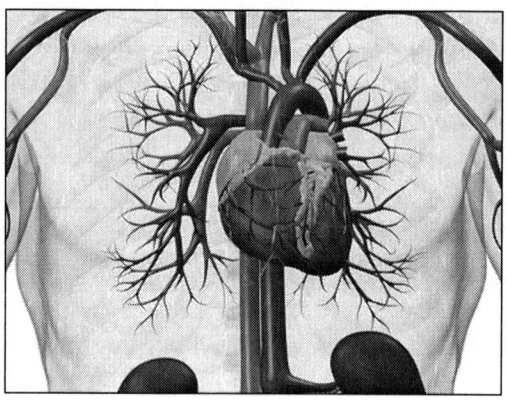

Figure 9: The seeds of the heart take root and the healthier the heart, the more robust the roots.

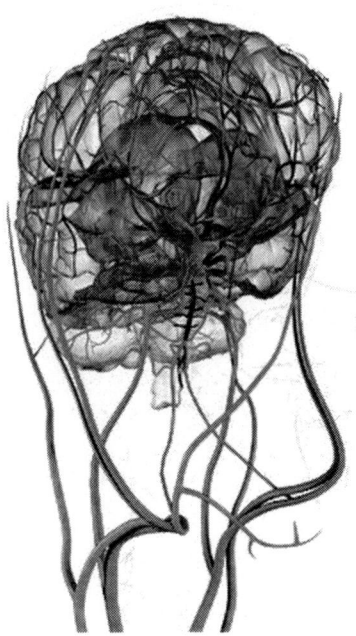

Figure 10: The main arteries flowing up the spine and entering the head and brain.

In Matthew 13 it speaks of the three different soil conditions in which a seed is planted, and what happens to each of them in each soil. Some seeds fell by the way side and the fowls came and ate them. Some seeds were planted on stony ground, having no root; they withered. Some were put in good soil and produced fruit up to a hundredfold.

The enemy comes to steal seeds from our heart that were put there by God. This is explained for us in Matthew 13:19: "When any one heareth the word of the kingdom, and understandeth it not, then cometh the wicked one, and catcheth away that which was sown in his heart. This is the person which received seed by the way side." Matthew 13: 22-23 says, "He also that received seed among the thorns is he that heareth the word; and the care of this world, and the deceitfulness of riches, choke the word, and he becometh unfruitful. But he that received seed into the good ground is he that heareth the

Hebrews 2:14: "Forasmuch then as the children are partakers of flesh and blood, he also himself likewise took part of the same; that through death he might destroy him that had the power of death, that is, the devil."

Chapter 5

Imagination

The heart is a much bigger deal than we ever imagined. Imagination comes from the root word "image." Our heart pumps blood. Blood holds images of our thoughts that come and reside in us as memories. It is the record keeper of all we experience. It stores images, not just audio (sound). Like little hologram pictures, science has discovered that all of creation has a picture of the whole in the tiniest cells of the whole.

There is scientific evidence now that shows the heart sends emotional and intuitive (spiritual) signals that helps direct our lives. The heart sends signals that align and direct systems within the body so they function in rhythm with one another. At the institute of HeartMath, founder Doc Lew Childre and scientists have found that the heart is capable of giving us messages and helping us far more than previously known.

Our hearts are capable of intelligently providing us with insight once the mind and emotions are balanced and become coherent— once we initiate that process. This intelligence is intuitive, a spiritual knowing that manifests in thoughts and emotions that are of value both to us and others. Blood vessels carry communication messages throughout the entire body, to keep everything in coherent rhythm, or in "sync." The body conserves energy that is vital to its growth and maintenance when our heart is operating in a state of coherency.

two gods operating within us at the same time. Whichever one we follow most in our thinking is the one we serve.

If you are negative, you can't be positive at the same time. If you go down, you cannot go up at the same time. The light is either on or it is off but darkness and light are not present at the same time. If a light is on in a room there is no darkness. The light provides growth, the darkness begins to kill.

God created you and me as an extension of Himself—to love. God cannot, *not* love Himself; He is the energy of love. We have some of Him in us; we were made in His image and likeness. This is why He cannot help but love you. He sees His love in you and there is no way He cannot love His own. He "IS" love. If you can really get this, you will begin to see why He forgives us of everything we do wrong when we ask Him and that He always loves us. It's why He can never leave us nor forsake us.

Judgment never came from God to wipe out any man, unless man became full of iniquities, full of sin. Not until evil sin had become part of the person—as it did in Satan and one third of the angels, to the point that they were totally consumed with it—did God do away with them in judgment.

Look at some of the things God says about our imagination in the heart:

Genesis 6:5: "And God saw that the wickedness of man was great in the earth, and that every imagination of the thoughts of his heart was only evil continually."

1 Chronicles 28:9: "And thou, Solomon my son, know thou the God of thy father, and serve him with a perfect heart and with a willing mind: for the LORD searcheth all hearts, and understandeth all the imaginations of the thoughts: if thou seek him, he will be found of thee; but if thou forsake him, he will cast thee off for ever."

1 Chronicles 29:18: "O LORD God of Abraham, Isaac, and of Israel, our fathers, keep this for ever in the imagination of the thoughts of the heart of thy people, and prepare their heart unto thee."

Genesis 8:21: "And the LORD smelled a sweet savour; and the LORD said in his heart, I will not again curse the ground any more for man's sake; for the imagination of man's heart is evil from his youth; neither will I again smite any more every thing living, as I have done."

Deuteronomy 29:19: "And it come to pass, when he heareth the words of this curse, that he bless himself in his heart, saying, I shall have peace, though I walk in the imagination of mine heart, to add drunkenness to thirst."

Proverbs 6:18: "An heart that deviseth wicked imaginations, feet that be swift in running to mischief."

Jeremiah 3:17: "At that time they shall call Jerusalem the throne of the LORD; and all the nations shall be gathered unto it, to the name of the LORD, to Jerusalem: neither shall they walk any more after the imagination of their evil heart."

Jeremiah 7:24: "But they hearkened not, nor inclined their ear, but walked in the counsels and in the imagination of their evil heart, and went backward, and not forward."

Jeremiah 11:8: "Yet they obeyed not, nor inclined their ear, but walked every one in the imagination of their evil heart: therefore I will bring upon them all the words of this covenant, which I commanded them to do: but they did them not."

Jeremiah 13:10: "This evil people, which refuse to hear my words, which walk in the imagination of their heart, and walk after other gods, to serve them, and to worship them, shall even be as this girdle, which is good for nothing."

Jeremiah 16:12: "And ye have done worse than your fathers; for, behold, ye walk every one after the imagination of his evil heart, that they may not hearken unto me."

Jeremiah 18:12: "And they said, There is no hope: but we will walk after our own devices, and we will every one do the imagination of his evil heart."

Jeremiah 23:17: "They say still unto them that despise me, The LORD hath said, Ye shall have peace; and they say unto every one that walketh after the imagination of his own heart, No evil shall come upon you."

Luke 1:51: "He hath shewed strength with his arm; he hath scattered the proud in the imagination of their hearts."

Romans 1:21: "Because that, when they knew God, they glorified him not as God, neither were thankful; but became vain in their imaginations, and their foolish heart was darkened."

Psalm 140:2: "Which imagine mischiefs in their heart; continually are they gathered together for war."

Proverbs 12:20: "Deceit is in the heart of them that imagine evil: but to the counselors of peace is joy."

Zechariah 7:10: "And oppress not the widow, nor the fatherless, the stranger, nor the poor; and let none of you imagine evil against his brother in your heart."

Zechariah 8:17: "And let none of you imagine evil in your hearts against his neighbor; and love no false oath: for all these are things that I hate, saith the LORD."

A Personal Testimony

I no longer doubt that God truly loves me, no matter what. I struggled with this my whole life. I didn't have a loving father or mother because they weren't shown love by their parents. If I can get you to see this like I saw it, you will no longer wonder if God loves you. Let me explain it in terms of energy power. God is not a being that we can see with our natural eyes (unless we would have walked on earth two thousand years ago). But before and after Jesus walked the earth, God is still who He has always been. He can never change. This doesn't mean that we can't feel Him like we can touch our close friends.

When God began to show me who He was and explain Himself to me through the invisible energies of everything, my eyes and heart were opened up to experience Him like never before. This is the way He revealed it to me and I will try to give a quick summary.

What and Who is God

God is massive powers of energy. All this energy isn't contained in one place or one body. He creates everything from the ultimate superpower of energy called love. The word tells us that He "IS" love. First John 4:8 tells us this: "He that loveth not knoweth not God; for God is love."

We are made from His energy. His energy is part of who we are. Just like your own children are parts of you and came from your energy make up, so we also came from God's energies. A part of Him is in us and we are made up of spirit, soul and body.

Romans 5:5 says, "And hope maketh not ashamed; because the love of God is shed abroad in our hearts by the Holy Ghost which is given unto us."

To say God does not love us—as so many believe because they have been programmed through man to believe they aren't lovable—is to say that God doesn't love. How can He not love when "love is" who He is?

When I realized this, I understood that there is no way He will not love me, unless I became as full of iniquity or sin, like Lucifer. This is everyone's individual choice, to resonate that completely with evil energy, or not. He gave us free will.

At what point does sin become full in a person? I believe that people who are beyond the point of repentance with God don't ask that question because they are no longer able to think that thought. They are that full of evil thoughts and sin's natures.

Our definition of love isn't the same as God's nature of love. It falls way short in the kind of power that love is expressed through God. His definition is in terms of everything being energy and God is all energies. It is not possible for Him to not love His own creation. A part of Him is in all creation and to not love all of creation would be God not loving a part of who He is. We are His children, the only living thing that has His Spirit in them. Only man was created in His Spirit and we have a spirit.

This is how I really came to know that I know He loves me—there is no way possible He won't love me. No matter how many times I fail Him, He created me to love. He will always be there, never leaving me because to leave me would be to leave Himself. I am created with a part of Him. He is inside of me. This verse in Romans makes more sense when you finally get it into your spirit.

Romans 8:39: "Nor height, nor depth, nor any other creature, shall be able to separate us from the love of God, which is in Christ Jesus our Lord."

This has caused me to believe in His love for me no matter what, in spite of how I am affected by the negative control system that Adam and Eve allowed to enter inside man's thinking at the fall. This also informed me why the first and second commandment is to love the Lord your God with all your heart, soul and mind, and then everyone else as yourself. Luke 10:27 says (my paraphrase); "If you can't love yourself or others, then you aren't loving God." Why, because we all have God's love energy within us all the way from the beginning of our existence.

I pray that this helps some of you who feel overwhelmed by the negative control system that tells you that you aren't loved, worthy, important enough, or that you have done too much wrong in your life for God to care about you, let alone love you. What you have done doesn't matter to God when you repent for your wrongs, from your heart. Jesus' death for our sins makes repenting from our own sin as simple as talking to Him in our head or out loud, saying to Him, "Please forgive me for my sins and show me who I really am—as you created me to be."

This is the number one problem for people. They don't have a picture of God that shows them He is love and is a good God.

Chapter 6

The Battle for the Heart

Looking more closely at the physiology of the heart will help us better understand how our enemy sets out to accomplish the task to contaminate our heart. Remember that this is what happened to Lucifer, turned Satan, when he hardened his heart to his Creator. He wants us to follow his path straight into his destiny.

Lucifer committed the ultimate sin all by himself, without anyone else teaching him how. He is the originator and producer of sin. When we sin, we never sin alone. Know this to understand the grace of God better and to know His love toward you. Every sin that man ever committed has always been done when joined with a spirit nature from Satan's kingdom of sin. The enemy and his kingdom are always together with us in the sin.

Only by God's grace and favor, which He gives to us freely, are we able to receive a removal of our sins. Jesus' blood cleanses and covers us. When we say yes to God and become a believer, we are washed and made whole through the blood that Jesus shed on the cross. Our sin is washed away at that very moment when we give our heart to the Lord. This is being born again. The blood cleanses us from the sin but we need the light of His word to heal the wounding caused by sin. It is two steps not one.

Ezekiel 36:26 says, "A new heart also will I give you, and a new spirit will I put within you: and I will take away the stony heart out of your flesh, and I will give you an heart of flesh."

At the fall in the garden, man's spirit died from being one with God's Spirit. Because they were one in spirit prior to the fall and sin, Adam instinctively knew what God's purposes were and flowed freely together as one spirit with God. Their energies flowed as one and in sync and harmony with each other. This was God's intention for man, to be one with Him.

I am not saying that man was equal to God and had God's fullness of Spirit. However, man's spirit and God's Spirit were effortlessly and instinctively one; man moved as one with God in spirit in all he did here on earth. That is until a breach of that unity in the spirit was caused by sin. This caused the dying process in man. Man was created without sin originally. Suddenly Adam and Eve saw differently than they ever had before. They saw their outward, physical self. This is why man covered himself and hid even from the voice of God. God's voice no longer had complete harmony with Adams spirit and sounded fearful to him, which is why he hid himself from God. He lost his spiritual ability to know God naturally and effortlessly. The spirit of man died.

Because of that breach, today we must seek after Him. Adam and Eve didn't need to seek His presence; they were in one accord with it all the time before sin entered them. They were without sin like God. The former harmony had become discord.

Once again, we have the Holy Spirit within our hearts enabling us to be connected with God in one spirit, because of Jesus' death on the cross. We need to learn to exercise our spirit to build a communication between us and God that was different for Adam and Eve once they sinned. We have to build the connection stronger and understand how to commune with God in a new form. The enemy makes the communication weaker and weaker through his deceptions, which causes discord within our operating systems.

The blood of Christ washes us, cleanses us from sin, and makes us whole without us sensing it through our five senses. Therefore it makes no logical sense. However, just because we don't see it, doesn't mean it isn't so. Do we see electricity flowing or gravity working? Do we all know how a caterpillar turns into a butterfly? Do we all know how our computer, in seconds, talks to another computer halfway around the world? No. But it still happens, doesn't it?

Our blood turns to J.C. (Jesus Christ) positive in a twinkling of an eye, when we turn and give our hearts to the Lord. It just does. Our spirit becomes reborn in Christ.

In Ezekiel 36:22-35, God tries to tell the Israelite's, through Moses, that He wants to restore them unto Him. Verse 26 speaks of a "new heart and a new spirit will He put within them." When we give our heart to the Lord, there is a transformation that takes place initially in our hearts. He washes our hearts clean of iniquities. Verse 27 says He will put His spirit within them. But we must understand that we must do our part to transform our minds. That requires exercise and effort on our part by putting the light of His word into us. This is referred to as the washing of the water of the word.

We have trouble believing because we don't understand how. And because we don't understand this, we end up being influenced by the enemy to keep going in sin. He knows what the blood of Christ can do to cleanse us and the light of the word of God we put in us, so guess what he sets out to do? You got it; he works even harder against us than before. Now we'll explore why that happens, what he is after in us, and how he can get it.

Notice the second half of the verse in 2 Corinthians 1:22 which says, "[He has also appropriated and acknowledged us as His by] putting His seal upon us and giving us His [Holy] Spirit in our hearts as the security deposit and guarantee [of the fulfillment of His promise]." He has a purpose and destiny He created each of us to fulfill in Him, before we were even conceived.

Each of us has a "hidden" treasure of potential within. It is up to each of us to choose to seek and uncover that. He gave us a free will to do with our time as we choose. However, if we don't seek to find it, we will die without discovering or fulfilling our purpose for being created. Us finding and fulfilling our purpose is a major threat to Satan and his kingdom. He is out to kill the Bride of Christ which is every believer (including you)! The potential of greatness is inside of you because that is where God positioned Himself, by sending the Holy Spirit to operate through you in the earth. He gave earth to man. (Read about this in Genesis 1.)

Just like Satan accessed the earth through Adam (a man), so must God access the earth through man. Why? He gave the earth to mankind to rule and reign in it.

Our free will is a choice given to us by God. It is an act that takes place in the heart of mankind. We don't become a believer and get grafted into His tree of life by just having our head say so. That decision must be made by our will, which comes from the heart, in order for it to be genuine, congruent, and in harmony with Jesus.

Picture it this way if you will. Let's imagine there are two waves on a piece of paper, running parallel with each other. Then remember that waves are energy moving. One wave is your spirit with negative thought and the other wave is the Holy Spirit. The stronger wave is the Holy Spirit inside your heart. Now imagine the wave of your negative thought to be erratic and choppy. That is, some high points to the wave are erratic, with some close together and others far apart. (See figure 11.)

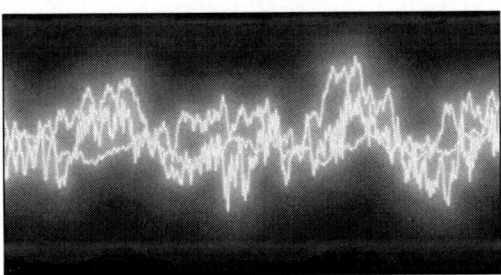

Figure 11: Your spirit wave with negative thought

Imagine the Holy Spirit wave of thought as steady and even—in high and low points. (See figure 12.)

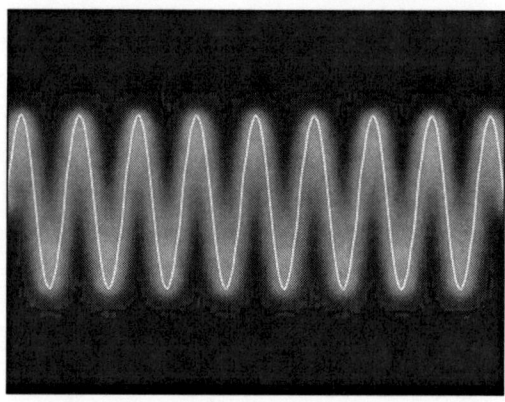

Figure 12: The wave of the Holy Spirit

Your free will determines if you want to say yes and yield in order to be in sync and congruent with the Holy Spirit wave. If you say no and stay incongruent, your energy wave stays erratic, and is inconsistent and out of sync with the Holy Spirit's wave. (See figure 13.)

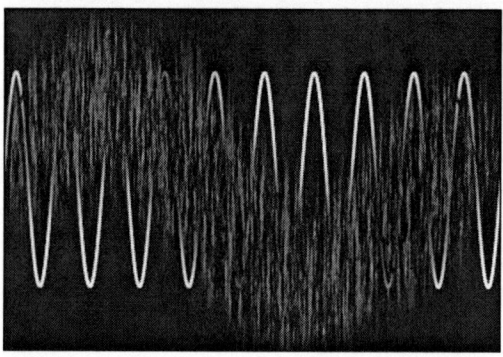

Figure 13: Your spirit wave, out of harmony with the Holy Spirit wave.

When you yield to the Holy Spirit, you have an energy output that becomes more energetic and more powerful. (See figure 14.)

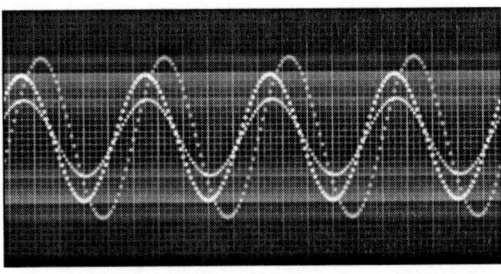

Figure 14: Your spirit in harmony with the Holy Spirit.

How is that? Let's say that the upper part of the wave is a plus 1 and the lower part of the wave is a minus 1. When we are in harmony with the wave, our upper part of the waving, being a plus one, joins the other wave of energy's plus one and becomes plus two. The bottom wave of energy for both is minus one, so when added together in congruency, becomes a minus two. This makes the wave double in strength and power.

Say there is an opera singer that hits a perfect sound wave of energy that measures plus one at the top and plus one at the bottom—matching the frequency of the wave of energy that forms the crystal glass. The glass shatters. Why? When her frequency, or wave of sound energy of plus one on top and plus one on the bottom matched the exact wave strength that was in the glass of crystal, her energy matched that of the glass and doubled its spin rate. Everything that exists is tied to a sound, to pitches.

What do I mean by "doubled"? All matter has spinning vortices of energy, spinning at certain set frequencies to form a visual of what you see as a physical structure. When the opera singers energy of plus one matched or came together with the plus one wave measure of energy, the vortices of energy began to spin twice as fast and shattered the glass. The glass could no longer stay together as a crystal glass because the opera singer changed its measurement of energy, thus changing its form. It no longer had a set of frequencies of energy that made it a crystal glass because the opera singer caused a doubling of spinning power of energies. This changed its frequencies from a crystal glass into a different set of frequencies which no longer were the frequencies that made up the form of a crystal glass. It could no longer hold together as a glass and shattered apart.

The opposite also can (and does) happen. If our waves of energy are incongruent, they cancel waves out. Let's say that you drop a pebble into a pond. (See figure 15.) You will notice the water ripples outward from where the stone entered the water. Those are energy waves, visible to see because they make the water move in waves.

Figure 15: A pebble thrown into water, releasing an energy wave which moves the water.

If you drop two pebbles in at the same exact time, you will notice that the ripples are taller since the wave of energy is stronger as it runs through the water. Where the ripples overlap, the combined power of the waves is doubled. This would be a harmonic resonance or you would say they are in congruency. (see Figure 16.) If you drop a pebble in first and another right after it, the second pebble will cause the ripple to flatten in the water or diminish. The second pebble thrown in canceled out the first pebble's energy wave because it wasn't in sync with its energy. One wave is going up when the other wave is going down. At the point where they converge these out of sync energy waves cancel each other out. The two energies did not run congruent with each other.

Figure 16: Ripples from each pebble converge on each other.

You may think that the water is moving and not a wave of energy moving through the water. A simple experiment will prove this. Put a fishing bobber into water, and then throw a stone into the water. Watch what happens. If the water was moving, the bobber would be carried out with the water ripples. Instead, the bobber rides the wave of energy to the top of the crest of the wave, then back down as the wave of energy passes by the bobber.

This is what happens when you choose to activate your positive control system of emotions. You become more energized and hold more power to stand up against the negative control system's influence. Why? Because you ride on top of the wave of the Holy Spirit, mirroring His power and energy—you are moving as one in Him. (See figure 14, page 71.)

This is what yielding your free will to God looks like. Can you imagine what your energies feel like when you are congruent, in harmony and in step with your heart, which is the throne room of the Holy Spirit? You ride on top of the wave of energy of the Holy Spirit. He makes it easy for you. Matthew 11:30 says it this way, "For my yoke is easy, and my burden is light."

Imagine your spirit being one rope, and the Holy Spirit is another rope. When you yield to the Holy Spirit inside of you, you wrap or braid yourself to Him and the two of you are flowing as one.

Chapter 7

Do Genes Control Us

This is a bigger thing than you ever realized because God writes your purpose, your future, your identity, and your destiny into the mind of the heart. These are the seeds He has planted in our hearts. The heart is a bed of soil with seeds deposited by God. God's word waters those seeds and fertilizes them, activating them to grow. God's word contains all life within it to grow mighty trees of righteousness.

What activates the growth of these seeds? We do, by making a choice to activate the positive control system inside of us. This system operates with all the natures that come from God: love, joy, peace, patience, forgiveness, kindness, gentleness, and more. This system is active in us when we focus on these things. We are watering our garden, planted in our hearts, with the thoughts we think in our minds. This is done by faith because faith is the substance of things hoped for and the evidence of things not seen (invisible).

Hope joins faith and love and acts as a sound generator. A generator, according to Webster's, "converts one form of energy into another, esp. mechanical energy into electrical energy, as a dynamo, or electrical energy into sound, as an acoustic generator."

Blueprints are located in DNA, deposited there by God when He created us uniquely and individually in His mind, from eternity. Then He put us into this time and space to fulfill something in His timing which has to do with the whole. He is the only one who sees the whole. We only see in part, according to what He chooses to reveal to us at different times.

You might believe God can do whatever He wants in this earth without us. Not so. God is very specific in what He says and does. He said in Genesis that He created the earth for man both to take dominion and multiply. Genesis 1:26, "And God said, Let us make man in our image, after our likeness: and let them have *dominion* over the fish of the sea, and over the fowl of the air, and over the cattle, *and over all the earth,* and over every creeping thing that creepeth upon the earth." He created earth FOR man to take dominion over.

God's blueprints are in the blood, and the heart pumps the blood that affects the rhythms and operations within us—extending even outside of us. The shed blood of Jesus was spilt on this earth to give man back the dominion over it that was lost in the Garden of Eden. When we tap into God (when we give our heart to Him in what is referred to as being born again), it is our moment of divine connection that uncovers the images (blueprints) of God, stored in our DNA. This is our own unique hidden treasure to uncover and put on display for God in the earth, known also as His glory.

Ecclesiastes 3:11 says, "He has made everything beautiful in its time. He has certain timing for everything. He also has planted eternity in men's hearts and minds [a divinely implanted sense of a purpose working through the ages which nothing under the sun but God alone can satisfy, yet so that men cannot find out what God has done from the beginning to the end" (AMP).

In order to get to your hidden treasure and become who God really intended you to be in His kingdom, you must choose to activate your positive control system. The seeds planted in the heart will not grow without you watering them to force production. This is what God meant by telling Adam and Eve to multiply in the earth. It is a multiplication of Himself in us. It is the glory (light) of Him that we carry inside of us, with which we walk around on earth.

This is when we may choose in our spirit to join the braided rope and ride the wave, to be in sync and harmony with the Holy Spirit, thus uncovering our hidden potential. To default to the negative control system will create negative manifesting natures of the enemy.

The discord of negative ruins the vibrations of God's perfect energy vibrations.

The word "uncover" is significant, especially as we explore more about our biology. Your DNA holds blueprints, pictures, seeds with images of what you look like in God's image and likeness (of what He had in mind when He decided to create you for His specific purpose). Can the DNA blueprint images that God placed in you be taken away from you by someone else? The images can become distorted by the choices we make or that our ancestors made. These are known as mutations or curses that have passed from previous generations to us.

Only about five percent of the human population is born with what is called "mutated" genes; genes that are dysfunctional. These people have something back in their generational line that causes the gene to be inherited. The other ninety-five percent of people are born with genes that aren't dysfunctional in any way. So if they become dysfunctional or mutated, it is because of something or someone in their environment programming them. It could also be their own thoughts causing distortions of energy, resulting in mutation.

DNA is a big deal. Even though science has proven that genetic determinism is invalid, they have continued to focus on the idea that genes control our lives. (We will explore this in more depth later.) They continue to say that we are stuck with what is in our genes because we inherited them and therefore, we are stuck with whatever diseases or negative behaviors they hold. This is not true.

We will get into detail about DNA a little later, but for now it is important to realize that our free will of choice is very powerful and we pretty much take it for granted, largely because we don't understand what it does to us on the inside. We don't understand our own physiology. We continue to explore our physiology now by taking a look at what we do when we choose to activate either our positive or negative emotional control systems.

Chapter 8

Activating Your Heart Intelligence

Your heart plays a bigger role than you imagine. When our thoughts activate the feelings of love, gratitude, giving, caring, and appreciation, it automatically causes a rhythm shift from our heart. This heart rhythm becomes more coherent the more we practice this thinking, creating both nerve impulses and chemical discharges within the body that affect every organ in a healthy, positive way. This only happens when we have engaged our positive control system with our thoughts. Keep in mind, this works in a negative way also.

When you activate your heart intelligence, meaning you willfully purpose to think on things above the horizon (thoughts that have light to them), you improve brain function, increase immunity, release stress relieving hormones, balance the autonomic nervous system, and lower the blood pressure because there is less stress on the heart. Your system comes into homeostasis.

This mental and physical system God gave us is far beyond amazing to comprehend. This is why it is vitally important to read the instruction manual, the Bible. Many people think that only guys are guilty of never reading the instructions. Not so. (I couldn't resist.)

Heart studies have shown that positive thoughts and feelings add positive energy to the systems of the body. Positive attitudes are positive emotions, expressing themselves through you from the inside to the outside. That is to say, positive attitudes are stored up "assets" of energy you carry on the inside that, when expressed by you, are coming from the inside to the outside of you, for everyone to see and feel. Whereas negative attitudes "deplete" our stored energies.

Envy, jealousy, and rage are examples of energy "deficits," as we know from what we have learned about emotional natures. They result from engaging our negative control system and can shut down our immune systems for up to six hours. This shows how negative energies cause our operating systems to become impaired. Left unchallenged over enough time can cause a complete shutdown of the organs and systems in our body.

The body is rewarded for exercising the positive control system of emotions by adding energy to the immune system, which adds hormones in balanced amounts to the body. The heart gets regenerated because it gets recalibrated to function as it was intended to function. Activating negative emotions drains these same systems.

What about non-productive thoughts? What kind of damage do they cause us, if any? That depends upon how emotionally charged with energy we make those thoughts. Emotions are the amplifier of our thoughts and how we perceive things in the world around us. We perceive thoughts that come into our mind according to beliefs we have built in previous situations.

Our head "reasons to know" but our heart "understands". We see this in Scripture. Job 17:4 says, "For thou hast hid their heart from understanding." Job 38:36 says, "Who hath put wisdom in the inward parts? or who hath given understanding to the heart?"

First Kings 4:29 says of King Solomon, "And God gave Solomon wisdom and understanding exceeding much, and largeness of heart, even as the sand that is on the sea shore." First Kings 3:12 says, "Behold, I have done according to thy words: lo, I have given thee a wise and an understanding heart." Psalm 49:3 says, "My mouth shall speak of wisdom; and the meditation of my heart shall be of understanding." Finally, Proverbs 15:14 says, "The heart of him that hath understanding seeketh knowledge:"

How we process things through our five physical senses affects what happens on the inside of us, and then on the outside of us. Your head won't take you where your heart will go. Your mind isn't big enough to wrap around what God is doing. Your heart will take you into revelation to renew your mind that your intellect won't allow you to go. By learning to follow your heart instead of your head, allows you to come out of the experience with understanding.

The brain in our head operates in a logical or linear fashion. It analyzes, memorizes, compares, and sorts communication. It matches this communication with previous similar events, and then converts that information into perception, thoughts and emotions. If the emotion is already there, it becomes more hard-wired into our fabric.

The heart, on the other hand, has been scientifically shown to communicate with the brain in four ways: through hormones (biochemically); through nerve impulses being transmitted (neurologically); through pressure waves (bio-physically), and; through electromagnetic field interactions (energetically).

When the heart beats, there are nerves that get activated that go to the brain. The brain of the heart detects hormonal information, pressure, and rate information. It translates and transmits this information into impulse messages, sent by way of the nerves. This information is sent from the heart to the brain by way of the vagus nerve and up the nerves in the spinal column. This information enters the brain in the medulla, located at the base of the brain. (See figure 17.) These messages then go farther up into the brain to influence the upper brain center's functions. These signals from the heart influence the brain to regulate many of the autonomic nervous systems signals that get sent out to blood vessels, glands, and organs.

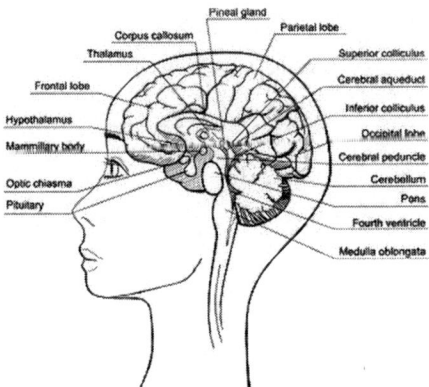

Figure 17: Parts of the brain

We are formed and fashioned in the image and likeness of God, and are therefore in part, a field of energy which transmits and receives. We have an output, and are an input of energy. God is so much energy that it is beyond our comprehension. Doctors know the heart transmits throughout the body a quality and pattern of energy via the heart's electromagnetic field. Think of how your cell phone works; it transmits information via an electromagnetic field. The heart's electromagnetic field is about five thousand times stronger in signal then the brain's field. The heart's energy output permeates every cell in our body. It resonates outside of us, detectable by magnetometers up to ten feet away.

Scientists have used a device called an electroencephalogram (EEG) to detect electrical information patterns in brain waves that are generated by the heart. This provides evidence that there is energy exchanged between the heart and the brain.

When we focus on our heart, that is when we focus on engaging our positive control system of emotional natures, the synchronization between the heart and the brain increases. So does our mental and physical well-being increase for the positive. Our thinking becomes sharper, our creativity and ideas increase, and we generate and move things into alignment and correction.

You could think of this like an orchestra joining together the many harmonious melodies and tunes to make a song that moves us. However, if half of the orchestra is playing one song and the other half is playing a different song, we would want to get up and leave because the sound disturbs us. This is what is happening on the inside of us. It has the opposite results when we think and engage the negative control of emotions causing discord in us—like the orchestra not playing together.

These emotional natures cause our operating systems to get out of synchronization and these rhythms cause poor mental function and distort the quality of output regulated from the brain that reaches our nerves, glands, and organs. This distortion from being out of harmony is the cause of all diseases—these are frequency problems.

Research evidence indicates that not only does this heart field resonate to our brain and different parts of our body, but the people around us can pick up on it. Ever wonder why you walk into a room and someone you come into contact with gives you a bad feeling, so you don't even speak to them? Perhaps you have experienced the opposite as well. You come into contact with someone for the first time and feel drawn to talk to them, and when you do, it feels as if you have known them for a lifetime. This is electromagnetic resonance in operation. You transmit your electromagnetic field all the time.

When we touch someone, there is an exchange of electromagnetic energy that takes place between the heart and the brain, shown to us by the electroencephalogram (EEG), a device that measures this. Our heart affects others around us and influences them. We shift to resonate with their energy and them with ours. These influences happen without our conscious awareness of it. We are either influenced by coherency or incoherency and the results from those energy transmissions go throughout our bodies. You could say we are either in harmony or discord with ourselves and others.

It would be nice to know that we are potentially transmitting a signal to that person's body that promotes health, as well as what we are receiving. We broadcast our emotional states all the time, as well as receive others. Oh, and yes, like attracts like. See why we can't bluff our enemy?

Chapter 9

How Separate Are We

The nuclear physicist Amit Goswami wanted to prove this, so he designed an experiment to prove that human behavior is influenced by quantum mechanical activities. He chose the principal called "nonlocality" in quantum physics. His research showed particles have a physical capability to become intimately connected, entangled with each other, once they touch one another. Energy exists not just in one place at one time, but everywhere all the time. This by the way was what Einstein referred to as nonlocality or, "spooky action at a distance."

Quantum physics has discovered that atoms are made up of subatomic particles— positive charged photons and negative charged electrons—which are like spinning tornadoes (called vortices) of negatively charged energy. (see Figure 18.) When these waves of energy touch and become entangled or intimately connected with one another, they act as one. So much so that when one of the pair changed its rotational spin, the other instantly changed its spin of rotation to compliment it.

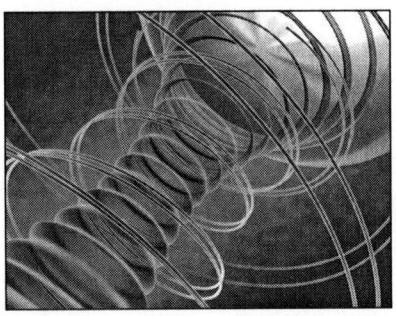

Figure 18: Spinning vortices of energy Illustrated

This happened even if the two particles were separated by a huge distance (as far away as totally opposite sides of the planet). How do you suppose the two are connected? By what or who are they connected?

Goswami set out to see if human brains could behave as entangled particles. If one subject's mind changed, would it cause the other subject's mind to change? The subjects were placed in electromagnetic, shielded Faraday chambers, fifty feet apart, where their EEG activity was monitored. He instructed pairs of subjects to interact by meditating on the same thing, which was to feel each other's presence at a distance. (see figure 19.) Gaswami flashed a strobe light into one of the subject's eyes, a distinctive electrical pattern that reveals the brain's response to a sensory stimulus. This is called an "evoked potential."

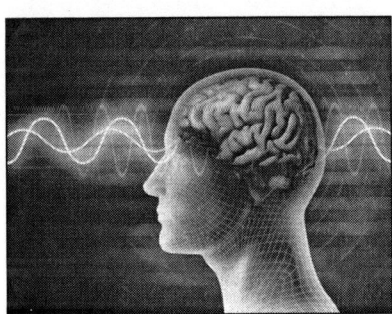

Figure 19: Transmitted energies of thought illustrated

While subjects were told to mentally engage in thought and to focus intently on feeling the other's presence, one subject was given an evoked potential, meaning that the flashing strobe light was used to create a response. Instantly, it induced an identical evoked potential, or the same response, from the partner who did not physically experience the stimulus (remember they were not even in the same place). This proves *that the activity in one person's brain can influence the activity in the brain of a separate entangled person.* How can this be explained?

There is only one connection that allows this law to operate. Who created the law? Who is everywhere, at all times without ceasing? There is a third party involved and it is the ever-present word, exuding from our Lord at all times.

Where in the Word is this illustrated?

Matthew 8:6-10, 13 says:

And saying, Lord, my servant boy is lying at the house paralyzed and distressed with intense pains. And Jesus said to him, I will come and restore him. But the centurion replied to Him, Lord, I am not worthy or fit to have You come under my roof; but only speak the word (the evoked potential), and my servant boy will be cured. For I also am a man subject to authority, with soldiers subject to me. And I say to one, Go, and he goes; and to another, Come, and he comes; and to my slave, Do this, and he does it. When Jesus heard him, He marveled and said to those who followed Him who adhered steadfastly to Him, conforming to His example in living and, if need be, in dying also], I tell you truly, I have not found so much faith as this with anyone, even in Israel. Then to the centurion Jesus said, Go; it shall be done for you as you have believed. And the servant boy was restored to health *at that very moment*. (AMP)

They were in two separate places, yet the change happened the very moment there was a harmonious connection from the centurion to Jesus to speak the very healing into existence at that very moment. The moment the Word was spoken, it evoked the response for which it was sent. It was the evoked potential, the introduced response.

But that was Jesus and He could do things we can't. Are you sure about that? Empower your life by allowing God to turn your thinking around. Jesus was showing us how to operate with a kingdom mentality, in kingdom laws that are in place. There were many times Jesus was frustrated with His disciples because they couldn't wrap their minds around what He was trying to teach them. He was speaking to their hearts, not their heads, but they were like us, conditioned by the world to overuse our heads. Besides, Jesus also said in John 14:12, that we shall do greater things than He did, "Verily, verily, I say unto you, He that believeth on me, the works that I do shall he do also; and *greater works* than these shall he do; because I go unto my Father."

Also think of what we are capable of, according to Deuteronomy 32:30, "How could one have chased a thousand, and two put ten thousand to flight, except their Rock (Jesus) had sold them, and the Lord had delivered them up?" (AMP) We can do this because we are entangled with our Divine creator.

We were created by Jesus' voice, the voice of the Word, in whom we live, move and have our being in Him. God is pure, extreme energy and is everywhere— omnipresent. You harmonize or resonate with His energy or with your enemy.

Acts 17:28 says just that, "For in him we live, and move, and have our being; as certain also of your own poets have said, For we are also his offspring." What are you sending to yourself and others around you? You resonate emotional natures from either the positive or negative control system within you. These systems, when activated, affect who you become. Our heart speaks a language from one of two sources. Matthew 12:34, "for out of the abundance of the heart the mouth speaketh." If you thought what you say comes from your mind, think again, it comes from your heart.

When hooked up to a heart rhythm monitor, one discovers that the slightest emotional changes show up immediately in the heart rate and the heart rhythm pattern. When we feel stressed, a disordered heart rhythm is created. This causes a reaction of change within our body. Blood vessels constrict or blood pressure rises.

When you experience this regularly, the result is hypertension (high blood pressure). The thing we need to know is that stress doesn't just pass through us like a fleeting mood but rather, it attaches itself and doesn't let go, resulting in changes to our physiology and health.

The exciting news is, if we control our negative emotions with positive ones, we can bring synchronicity and rhythm back to our system, resulting in balance and order. During those times of stress, which involve concentrating too much on negative emotions, if we will shift our thoughts to emotions of gratitude, thankfulness, caring and love. We can bring our physiology back into alignment and homeostasis (balance).

If you choose to think about something totally, not even related to the thing causing you stress, you can bring rhythm back. Think of your new baby, your grand kids, or some happy recent event and feel it with your heart, those warm fuzzy feelings in your memory. Focusing on something totally unrelated to what is causing you stress shifts your emotional resonance output. It brings good rhythm to your cardiovascular efficiency and balances your nervous system. This is proven biological science that works off the principals set forth in the word of God.

Entanglement

It works just like this example. When you fill a room with pendulum clocks and start them all swinging differently, you might think that they will each keep the same rhythm that you started them with. Wrong. Given time, they will all swing to one unified rhythm. What determines which rhythm they will all swing to? The clocks will all come into synchronicity with the clock that has the strongest rhythm. This is known as "entrainment."

The heart is the strongest oscillator of the body, like the strongest clock in the example, and the heart pulls the rest of the body systems into entrainment with its rhythm. This means that when we are in a state of deep love or gratitude, the brain synchronizes in harmony with the state of the heart, and then every other operating system of the body follows. Think of how your heart feels when you first fall in love, or when your first baby is born.

We alter our emotional states. No one except us can control our emotional nature. The challenge we face is getting the brain in our head to surrender to the heart long enough to make a connection with the intelligence of the heart brain. The brain in our head becomes familiar with certain modes of operation, such as stored memories.

Remember the trees of righteousness in our brain. This is where the greater number of stronger branches we have developed from emotions stored above the light of the horizon which allows us more flexibility to shift and make other connections more easily. The fewer branches we have that are deeply embedded with the same negative emotional memories, the harder it is for us to make a shift to connect with our heart. These old neurological patterns are embedded by years of habits. When these pathways are challenged, they hold on stubbornly. Remember, these are the pathways that, when threatened with change, begin to fire on their own, out of habit. We must not pay them any attention or we will reactivate them.

So what does this sound like to you? The heart will send you a clear signal with the feeling of "don't do this." You will hear your head demanding to know the logical, linear explanation of the why, how, what, and when of not doing what you have always done before. When these thoughts persist in your head, and they will, the wrong thing to do is justify and rationalize the thing your heart is telling you not to do. Your head will persuade you not to change, but you lose the connection you heard from your heart. (see figure 20.) I think of the cell phone commercial that says, "Can you hear me now?" You must allow your head to move toward the signal transmitting from your heart.

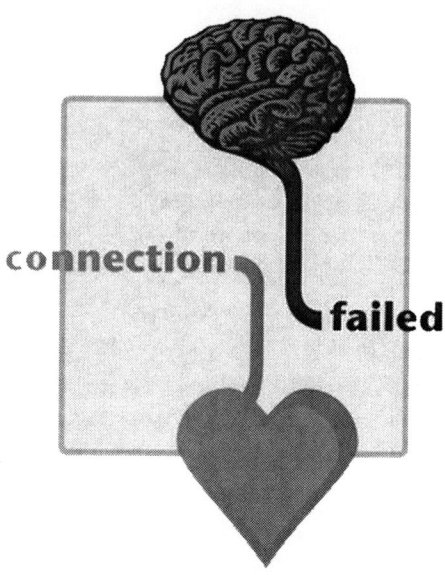

Figure 20: Non-congruency between the heart and the head illustrated

If the vast majority of our reactions to life are dictated from our head and logic, and we do not allow our heart to join our intelligence, we become double-minded and unstable in our ways. If we get our head in sync, or in rhythm with the most powerful oscillating force in our body (our heart), we become single-minded because the two are working as a team.

Who do you think tells us to forget what our heart says? Our enemy! We already know that the throne room for our God connection is in our heart. (Do you see now what is happening to you and why?)

To make a distinction between the head and our heart can fool us at first. Things from the heart express themselves with more authenticity, are void of expectations, and are unconditional. The more we do things that come from our head, the more we do things with emotional attachments and conditions. The head is expectation driven. To involve your heart requires mature emotion management in order to manifest the qualities of the heart with any consistency.

In managing our emotions, we stop and concentrate on the still small voice of the heart and we see a bigger perspective. This result of stopping and learning to check in with our heart can keep us from pain and hurts. Most of our pain comes from our expectations not being met.

Most of the time, we think just the opposite and don't want to get our hearts involved because we have been hurt when we have put them out there. As a result, many of us have done the deadly thing of building walls around our hearts.

We can understand the operations of our heart and learn to follow it by thinking back on the last time we gave your heart to someone and got hurt. (I can hear some readers saying that the last time they followed their heart about a relationship or business deal, they got burnt.) This is our enemy's playground of happiness.

Unfulfilled Expectations from our Head

The bigger question to ask ourselves is how our heart was affected when we did what we did. What type of heart did we follow? The true heart is pure in intention without a head full of expectations and conditions. We follow our heart, and know we are doing so, when our head doesn't have emotional expectations. How can we tell if that is what we did? We must ask ourselves if the pain and hurt was caused by the love we felt (heart), or by hopes and conditions that weren't met for us (head)? Therein lies the answer to know how much the head got in the way of a heart message.

There is no pain and hurt in pure love. Pain and hurt comes from unfulfilled expectations that we put upon people and circumstances. When our expectations were not met, we got hurt. The result ends up with us being fearful of doing things which involve the heart. Yet this is the opposite of what the word tells us. First John 4:18 says, "There is no fear in love; but perfect love casteth out fear: because fear hath torment. He that feareth is not made perfect in love." We fear because we have been taught our whole life to do so and to expect certain outcomes in situations.

When our system is coherent, we waste none of our energy and our power is flowing in harmony. Circumstances are created by our enemy to steal our coherency. Emotional natures from above the light of the horizon create coherency within the body. Lack of coherency affects our mental clarity, how long it takes us to react to things, our ability to listen and hear, our level of sensitivity, and our state of being.

We have the choice to keep putting up with stress (thoughts and emotions that aren't managed by us), or we can take responsibility to change our emotional natures and how they get expressed through us. Stress enters any situation we come into by having a perception of the situation that doesn't meet our expectations. Then we don't manage how we react to those situations. Stress is an unmanaged reaction to a stimulus that has come into our field of awareness.

Resistance to Opposing Energies

This causes us to get out of sync and our energy literally feels like tension or frustration, and we feel resistance to that energy to the point where it becomes disabling. These are all energies converging with lack of proper management, and often, lack of identification. The two systems that react to this are the central nervous system and the hormonal or biochemical system. Excess cortisol (a hormone), is dumped into our system and because of the repeated level of stress, the brain must be able to handle what isn't turning off, so it resets to have the body maintain a higher level of cortisol production. From that point forward, the brain believes that the new high is normal.

With a continuation of the new "normal highs" of cortisol come impaired memory and learning, because the excess cortisol destroys brain cells. It also weakens the immune system, affects metabolism, increases bone loss, reduces muscle mass, and disturbs glucose regulation, to name a few. Over time the body can only take so much and, like rotting wood on a pillar that holds a roof up, it will break down at the moment it loses stability.

Our bodies don't care if we are right or wrong, only our thoughts in our mind do. In your mind you may feel justified for getting angry with someone, but the only place you feel good is in the head. The body's immune system shuts down for six hours due to a three minute angry outburst and you think you are right for having gotten angry? It's only in your head. You pay the price for needing to be right in your body. During this disorder, the heart is transmitting an incoherent signal, not only to our body but to the space around us as well.

Chapter 10

You Are a Transmitter and a Receiver

"Spectral analysis" determines which individual frequencies make up an electrical signal. A spectrum analyzer, or spectral analyzer, is a device used to examine the spectral composition of some electrical, acoustic, or optical waveform. It is like putting a spice mix into a machine and it tells you what ingredients it has. It is from this information that the amount of coherence in the heart's electrical energy output can be determined, going both to the cells in our body, and to people in our field.

Your perception affects the signals of your heart. It really isn't the cause of the stress but how we perceive the cause. This is good news because it tells us that the cause doesn't need to keep eliciting the same response from us. We can control our reaction to it by changing our perception of the event. This is why the same identical event can bring a high level of stress to one person, and none to another. So stress starts with perception. Our perceptions come from stored beliefs.

We can shift our perception and alter our reaction by learning how to shift from our head to our heart. We have been given the power and choice to think our way into despair, or to stop the process by dwelling more on the emotions of light above the horizon. This keeps the power that comes from old mindsets and emotional natures below the horizon from taking us over.

When we learn to pay more attention to our heart and its intelligence, we can change our moods. Moods come from emotions. We can do this by sincerely making the choice to focus our heart on feeling emotions like love, gratitude, and caring. Philippians 4:8 says it this way, "Finally, brethren, whatsoever things are true, whatsoever things are honest, whatsoever things are just, whatsoever things are pure, whatsoever things are lovely, whatsoever things are of good report; if there be any virtue, and if there be any praise, think on these things." Doing this has a physical effect on our bodies.

Luke 21:14 says, "Settle it therefore in your hearts, not to meditate before what ye shall answer." This scripture tells us there is a difference between meditating in your mind and meditating with your heart. We are to use our hearts when meditating to cause synchronization between our heart and mind. This brings coherency throughout our cells, causing mental clarity.

There are many meditation techniques that teach one to focus in the head, the crown area, or the forehead. They condone using the mind to quiet the mind. This is what most of us have been programmed to do, without knowing what we are doing wrong. The mind is full of linear and logical thinking.

Research has shown that there are changes in brain waves (frequencies) and autonomic reduction, but they rarely (if ever) produce coherence in heart rhythms. Some of those techniques have you focus on the heart; however the energy of the mind is often directed there. We must start in the heart; engage those feelings from the heart feeling them. This allows the heart to distribute the energy necessary for synchronization throughout. It is the difference between thinking with your mind that your sister's baby is precious and "feeling" your own baby is precious. Feel where the emotions came from when you thought about that statement. Find strong feelings that engage your heart to move and not just your head. Meditate on those things.

Your State of Being

This is the type of meditation that the Word tries to indicate we do dwelling upon the goodness of God, all that He has done for us, and how He made us. Why? Little did we know that to think and follow the intelligence in our heart affects our entire being for good or bad. As we do this, we synchronize our heart with our mind, causing us to find inner peace and harmony, allowing us to hear God more clearly. The messages from your heart become clearer when the mind is quiet. This neutralizes the mental and physical effects of stress upon us. Love, in place of stress, becomes your new state of being.

There is a shift that takes place within you when you practice this over time—a shift you actually feel. There is also improved health and well-being. After a while you will find it uncomfortable, not being connected to your heart. When you react from your head only, it won't feel right. Even others around you that are reacting from their head will stand out to you. Remember to love them. You didn't always know what to do. They are where you used to be.

Creating coherence between your heart and head puts power in your life. The head notices what needs changing, but the heart (the largest oscillator of the body), is the powerhouse to bring you changes that you thought were impossible. Be sure our enemy knows this as well and fights to cause breakdowns in our bodies. But he is the weaker power by far.

The state of our mental and emotional management "diet" determines our health far more than the food we eat. We consume like energy every second of every day. Thoughts and feelings turn into emotions. The body was fully designed to equip us with adequate energies to confront and defeat our stresses.

When we allow our energies to direct our thoughts toward negative emotions, we deplete our energy supply and long-term we deplete our energy reserves, causing our bodies to become diseased. The repair and replacement for most cells is diminished, if not halted, over long periods of time and continued stress. Our immunity becomes too weak to handle the overload that has been created in our system and this causes our DNA to become altered, causing even more destruction.

When we make the choice to put the electrical energy of our heart to work for us, we effectively plug the energy leaks by choosing positively charged emotions from our heart which results in our entire system aligning with the energy from those emotions. We begin to feel more energized and less fatigued and worn out. There is less tension and drag between the two branches of the autonomic nervous systems. There is less wear and tear right down to the cellular levels throughout our body. There are psychological nutrients of energy being managed for optimum performance to our physiology.

Nothing happens without energy. Nothing exists without energy sustaining it. When we understand this, we can create and cause our energy to work for us, instead of against us. It is within our ability to manage ourselves. Every thought and emotion impacts our energy supplies flowing in and out of our reserves. It requires that we notice the processes of judgments, unforgiveness, anger, and worry. When they happen, we purpose to consciously replace them with love, caring, appreciation, compassion, and more. These emotional natures are very potent.

Unforgiveness, bitterness, anger and resentment cause chemicals (acids) which eat away at the heart, leaving scar tissue that hardens the heart. Unforgiveness is the number one negative emotion people carry in them. Think of what it can do to you. We tend to think we are hurting the other person when we choose not to forgive. Unforgiveness is a lie from the enemy. It completely breaks our system down because we are generating the energy of unforgiveness. All energy that we give focused thought to has to run through us. This is why we are to forgive, because unforgiveness brings death to our physical body. It doesn't matter if we were in the right, it will kill us and not the person we choose not to forgive.

In how many places does the word of God talk about the heart becoming hardened? Did you ever think it was literally scarring the tissues of your physical heart? The word has been given to protect us from what our enemy wants to do to us.

Managing Emotions and Memory Storage

Emotional natures from below the horizon are more likely to occur when our heart and head are not aligned with each other. The more they are aligned, the easier it is for us to feel emotions like love, appreciation and understanding.

The heart is the most powerful change agent in all of the body. Why? Messages from the heart find their way to the amygdala, the area in the brain below the frontal lobe. As the heart rhythm changes, so does the electrical activity in the cells of the amygdala, causing it to synchronize to the heartbeat. This can be the cause for positive changes in perception when heart rhythms become more coherent.

The amygdala (located deep in the center of the brain) is a processing center our brain uses to assign emotional significance to what we hear, see, smell and touch. It is influenced by input from the heart and information from our cerebral cortex, the top upper region of the brain. Neuroscientist Dr. Karl Pribram, in his book, *Brain and Perception* explains how the amygdala compares what's familiar in memory with new information coming into the brain. If an old emotion has become familiar, we respond to new and familiar situations with the same emotion, even if it doesn't make sense to do so.

Justifying Negative Emotions Hurts Us Not Them

Justification is the number one reason why people don't manage their emotions. Justification tells us that we only need to manage emotion we want to express under certain circumstances. It tells us that the anger we displayed toward someone was understandable, based on what they did or said to us. It says that if we have anger with good reason, we don't need to control that anger. Whether understandable to our way of reasoning or not, it just isn't worth the energy output that it costs our system to lose.

Anytime we rationalize our negative emotional output, it directs our energy to be spent on hurting, fearing, feeling guilty or betrayed — and this keeps us wounded. Why? We are generating the energy that causes the chemicals and nerves to overload our system. These emotions remain trapped for a long time because we continually justify them to ourselves. The *"tap" of poisonous toxins is left open by our choice*. It's not the problem that causes energy drain as much as the significance we keep assigning to the problem. *Emotions are energy in motion!* What is the motion you want to assign?

Scientists studying brainwave activity has confirmed that our emotional reactions show up before we have a thought about them. We perceive, evaluate it emotionally, and think about it afterward. The energy from our emotional natures operates at a higher speed than our thoughts. The invisible world of emotional natures travel at a higher speed than our mind works. Our conscious mind processes 40 bits of information per second. Our non-conscious processes 40 million bits of information per second.

When our heart is more in alignment with our mind, our spiritual intuition gives us clearer direction on how to manage our emotions and feelings, before we invest our energy in them. Emotions were given to us so we could express a nature to others and ourselves. All emotions have a certain nature to express, good or bad. When we aren't in alignment and in balance with our heart, the mind can use our emotional energy to express a reaction to how it perceives. This is why thoughts that are not held captive, but allowed to fly out without controls, are escaping energy that drains us.

We often feel emotions, not understanding why. Emotional natures travel so fast that even when we try to manage our reaction to them, we find that we can't because they happen too fast for our mind to reason. The logical, linear mind doesn't have the ability to intercept these emotions to help create a more positive result. This is why so many people say "I can't help it." What one needs to understand is this: *Unmanaged or mismanaged thinking, plus the power of emotions, equals a battlefield in your mind. You are a "house" divided against itself and war rages inside of you.*

This happens because the mind isn't coherent from the heart. Emotional energy has been activated and that energy won't settle down until it gets orders to do so from the heart. The heart rhythm is the only source for coherence, bringing your activated energies into balance and alignment.

You may have an argument with someone and apologize afterward for what you didn't mean to say. It may take you twenty-four hours to stop feeling bad on the inside of you for what happened. You may even try to convince yourself that all is okay, without success. This emotional drain continues to deplete your energies and you can't turn it off. In fact, an overactive mind, without your heart directing things, is how strong opinions are developed. You develop rigid mindsets that look like deep ruts inside your brain.

One way to tell if you are allowing heart intelligence to connect with your thinking is to evaluate *how neutral you are about your opinions.* Strong opinions come from attaching similar perceptions to stored memories. This is why rigid mindsets are formed. The mind in our brain alone can't bring order to our being. The heart doesn't think so linearly, it provides awareness to situations that are needed to become more neutral about what you are experiencing. The heart allows for unthought of possibilities that can provide information to allow you to perceive differently than your thoughts told you. The heart is required to bring coherency.

People believe that they can think their way into a changed attitude (an attitude is an emotion being expressed). Positive emotional changes require heart coherence. This requires action on our part, with consistent practice. Many of our emotional responses are stored in our cells from past experiences, locked into our nerve cells and the circuits they have formed.

Our locked-in memories (and current thoughts) affect our current perceptions, which in turn affect our body's biochemical hormone production and neurological commands. This is why, even if we can't recall a previous experience, it can still influence our current behavior. The more we repeat an action or behavior, the stronger the connection that is made. Short-term memory makes a temporary connection, not hard-wired in, because the synapse strength isn't strong enough. It becomes stronger and gets hard-wired as long-term memory when the nerve cells do two things.

First, when a molecule is formed that turns on a gene contained in the DNA of a cell. This is caused by a chemical reaction produced when we think with repetition on the same thoughts. Secondly, when the nerve cell changes and grows in structure. This change to the nerve cells cause the circuit to become hard-wired with those emotional responses, repeated behaviors and emotional attitudes we express. A strong emotional stimulus releases hormones and neurotransmitters which help imprint that emotional memory into our neural circuits.

These memories get remembered in order of importance. The *greater remembrance goes to negative emotional states over positive ones.* That's why you have heard that it takes ten positive statements to override a negative one. The problem with that is we tend to voice the negative far more than we voice the positive, leaving us filled up with negative comments.

We can reduce emotional and hormonal impact upon our system by becoming more heart coherent. We must pay attention to what is running our body. Remember, all negative emotions generate energy that is incoherent. Positive emotions generate coherency to your system.

The idea is to bring balance and peace to our operating system. That is only attainable by involving our heart. It changes things for us mentally and physically.

Intent is a Strong Force

Intent carries energy of purpose to something we project. It is a strong force within us. Our intent carries the authority of the name of Jesus that we have when we become a part of the Bride of Christ. Intent carries our heart to connect and entangle with God's heart and others. Intent comes from a sincere, clear desire of the heart.

Jeremiah 30:24 says, "The fierce anger of the LORD shall not return, until he hath done it, and until he have performed the intents of his heart: in the latter days ye shall consider it." Hebrews 4:12 says, "For the word of God is quick, and powerful, and sharper than any two edged sword, piercing even to the dividing asunder of soul and spirit, and of the joints and marrow, and is a discerner of the thoughts and intents of the heart." Jeremiah 30:24 says, "The fierce anger of the LORD shall not return, until he hath done it, and until he have performed the intents of his heart: in the latter days ye shall consider it."

Think about when you were told by your parent to apologize to someone you wronged. If you were like most kids, the apologies came from the head most of the time. But when you involved your heart, there was coherency to the apology. It even sounded and felt different. The cells of our body know the difference and our heart knows the difference if we pay attention.

When we add a focused intent to an emotion we express, it gives more power to that emotion, adding more energy to it. It is the same reason a laser beam has more power than a fluorescent light bulb.

Without intent behind what we express and clear purpose to change, the lower the benefit for us.

Intent carries a strong belief from the heart to accomplish a cause. It projects something with a purpose in mind. It adds meaning and significance to focus your energy like a laser toward a target. With intent, you have authority to call your next nanosecond to be in a specific way for your future. The authority is in you to cause to be, that which you see. The "double slit experiment in physics proves it is what you observe that you cause to be. You do this with your intent, coming from your sincere desire and with your observation.

Be careful how you observe your circumstances and life. You are causing things to be. Science gives evidence to what the Bible has told us all along.

When He walked the earth, Jesus could tell the difference within people, if their thoughts were congruent from their heart to their head. That is why He responded to some and ignored others. He could tell who was coherent from the heart. He said the thoughts of men were located in their hearts. He didn't look to their heads for their thoughts.

Luke 9:47: "And Jesus, perceiving the thought of their heart..."

Luke 5:22: "But when Jesus perceived their thoughts, he answering said unto them, What reason ye in your hearts?"

Matthew 9:4: "And Jesus knowing their thoughts said, Wherefore think ye evil in your hearts?"

Matthew 15:19: "And Jesus knowing their thoughts said, Wherefore think ye evil in your hearts?"

Mark 7:21: "For from within, out of the heart of men, proceed evil thoughts..."

Luke 2:35: "(Yea, a sword shall pierce through thy own soul also,) that the thoughts of many hearts may be revealed."

Luke 24:38: "And he said unto them, Why are ye troubled? and why do thoughts arise in your hearts?"

(Note: All verses shown above are from the original King James Version. That version is the closest translation to the original Hebrew. Other translations translate "heart" as "mind.")

Mark 5:31 says, "And his disciples said unto him, Thou seest the multitude thronging thee, and sayest thou, Who touched me?" How do you think Jesus could tell who touched Him? The intent of this woman was identified by Jesus because this woman's congruent heart drew the energy from Jesus and He could tell that someone had pulled energy from Him with their strong, focused intent.

Quantum Entanglement

It has been discovered in quantum physics that information is exchanged instantly through what they call *"quantum entanglement."* Physicists have found that *once two particles touch, they remain interconnected and cannot be disconnected.* Your body is made up of electrons so tiny, you can't see them. Quantum entanglement revealed that when you change even one particle, the other particle, even if located miles away, will change simultaneously. This means that when we hear frequencies of information that impact our thoughts, that information remains connected to us.

What this suggests is that the power of our thoughts, emotions, and words are greatly interconnected between us and other people. All of these thoughts of information flow in and out of us. What are we saying to each other, out of ignorance and lack of knowledge that is bad? Consider what and how the enemy uses this knowledge.

This also brings up the entanglement we have with our Creator and God. We are connected Spirit (God) to spirit (man) and spirit-man to spirit-man. When you pray for someone, you transmit your intent and they receive it. The two of you are entangled, hook up, and cannot be disconnected. You are hooking up where your intent is transmitted. This is the invisible world we are talking about—the world we take for granted because we don't observe what is happening there by our five senses. But that doesn't make it non-real. The invisible world is more real than the physical world. All things coming into our world come from the invisible realm.

So is prayer a thing of the flesh, or of the spirit? You can pray from the flesh with intelligent words, but the true power of prayer is found when you pray in the spirit. Your heart has an intent that your mind doesn't know. When your spirit is engaged in your prayers, that is when you hook up. Your heart is the throne room for the Holy Spirit and your spirit is seated in heavenly places—hooked up—both here and there. Yes, you are in two places at once. It has been discovered that we literally are blinking in and out of this world. (We explore more about that science discovery a little later.)

Your spirit and the Holy Spirit radiate or resonate from your heart. So when your spirit prays, you hook up to who you are praying for, and the Holy Spirit is hooked up as well, just as in the story of the centurion and Jesus. In Matthew 8:8, the centurion asks Jesus to speak a word to heal his servant, telling Jesus that He didn't have to go to where the servant was. "The centurion answered and said, Lord, I am not worthy that thou shouldest come under my roof: but *speak the word only,* and my servant shall be healed." Then in Matthew 13:8, we read what the result was: "And Jesus said unto the centurion, Go thy way; and as thou hast believed, so be it done unto thee. And *his servant was healed in the selfsame hour."* He was healed in the very moment of time that Jesus spoke the word.

Your intent carries the authority of the name of Jesus that you have as the son or daughter of Christ, as the Bride of Christ. When man intercedes to the Lord, he is hooked up to Him. This is why the power of unity is so strong and disunity brings such disconnect.

You might be thinking you shouldn't have hooked up with somebody, so now what do you do? First John 4:4 says, "Ye are of God, little children, and have overcome them: because greater is he that is in you, than he that is in the world." You have the greater power within you over the enemy. Use your authority and intent wisely. You must make a right connection in the Lord to disconnect from your enemy. You must plug into the greater power. Divine power is the only power that renders the enemy powerless.

Our enemy senses energy resonating from us like light bulbs having different watts. He is like the dimmer switch on the wall that is used to reduce light gradually when it is too bright in the room. He continues to dial down the light radiating from our heart by serving us lies through thoughts he puts in our minds. We think that we can bluff him but we cannot. Nor should we fear him because he isn't the one with the greater powers of energy. He is the weaker one. Learn how to use your authority to overcome his tricks.

Lucifer was the bearer of light. He housed all energy and was full of wisdom, knowledge, and was in charge of its operation. He was never the original source of it. He knew all about frequencies of energy. Lucifer witnessed all of creation as it was created. He saw and studied how man was created. He was the covering for all creation. He lost his upper bandwidth of energy in the judgment of God. He lost his position. But that doesn't mean he forgot what he had.

He doesn't have the capability to operate in that flow of energy he once had. He now tries to steal our energy by distorting it to slow down his day of judgment. Our time and energy is what he is after for his goal is to destroy the Bride of Christ. That light we carry is the glory of God inside of us.

When we are under pressure, feel overwhelmed or edgy, are under time restraints, or frustrated, we are spinning our wheels and going nowhere fast. What's worse, is this begins to feel like the same thing over and over each day of the week. When we are overwhelmed and edgy we have to regroup at some point; pick up the pieces, or lose vast amounts of time and energy.

You can create a time shift within yourself when you stop in wheel-spinning moments and check in with your heart, and purpose to think about the emotions above your light horizon. What you will find is that it brings you back to emotional balance. Your time is better spent from that moment forward and you save a great deal of time and energy for yourself, rather than expending it on keeping you out of balance and causing you to leak energy. This stops a chain reaction that is causing you to lose time and energy, shifting you into a zone that results in your energy and time serving you with effective results, both mentally and physically.

You move through life at the most efficient speed when you are balanced internally. Why? You are congruent, which equals stronger energies of light and life running through your body. You will notice a clearer head of intelligence, causing more proficiency, less procrastination, and having more empathy for others—all of which improve your communication and relationships.

Your environment shifts around you. Don't forget, you resonate outward into your environment. Think about the person that seems to be up all the time, full of energy and smiling. These people have learned consciously, or non-consciously, to live with their thoughts pulling emotional natures from above their horizon.

Emotional natures from below the horizon are energy suckers that zap your energy, snuffing your light out. The opposite is true of emotional natures from above the horizon. They are full of energy and are full of light and life.

It is the enemy that schemes to use the knowledge of evil to cause us to operate emotionally from below the horizon where it is dark, to cause a hardening of our heart. Deuteronomy 11:16 says, "Take heed to yourselves, that your heart be not deceived, and ye turn aside, and serve other gods, and worship them." Look what was said about Satan's heart, for which God judged him:, "Thus saith the Lord GOD; Because thine heart is lifted up, and thou hast said, I am a God, I sit in the seat of God, in the midst of the seas; yet thou art a man, and not God, though thou set thine heart as the heart of God" (Ezekiel 28:2). "Ezekiel 28:6 records: "Therefore thus saith the Lord GOD; Because thou hast set thine heart as the heart of God." Isaiah 14:13 says, "For thou hast said in thine heart, I will ascend into heaven, I will exalt my throne above the stars of God: I will sit also upon the mount of the congregation, in the sides of the north..."

Stop underestimating your enemy. He speaks through your mind to lead you down the same path he took, which is to take thoughts to create emotional natures of distortion and incoherency, which will change the condition of your heart. He comes into our mind to get to our heart, to spiritually change its condition, which in turn also changes its physical condition.

So when we get hurt and want to shut our heart down in order to protect ourselves from what we think is hurtful and tormenting, the ultimate deception that we don't recognize is that we aren't protecting our heart at all. We are in fact doing exactly what the enemy wants us to do—close ourselves off and separate from those around us we perceive are hurting and wounding us. We agree with what he says is causing our wounding.

Strongholds of the Mind

Thoughts in the mind create emotional strongholds in our brain. Thoughts carry a nature which is either good or bad. Those natures affect the condition of our heart. In which kingdom of emotional natures do you want to participate?

We can't look to man to define our identity of who we are on the inside. The world system teaches us to do this from birth, onward. First, man doesn't know because man didn't create man. Second, men are listening to the same voices you have been and are deceived in the same ways. This is why we can't possibly fight carnal nature flesh with carnal nature weapons.

We have to get a clear definition of our identity and purpose from the Lord who created us. When we do, the weapons we carry within us are mighty to the pulling down of evil strongholds. Second Corinthians 10:4 says, "For the weapons of our warfare are not carnal, but mighty through God to the pulling down of strong holds." Love is a mighty weapon that overcomes death. Song of Solomon 8:6 says, "Set me (God) as a seal upon thine heart, as a seal upon thine arm: for love is strong as death."

Be careful what you believe because belief comes out of the heart. Acts 8:37: "And Philip said, If thou believest with <u>all</u> thine heart, thou mayest. And he answered and said, I believe that Jesus Christ is the Son of God."

Romans 10:9: "That if thou shalt confess with thy mouth the Lord Jesus, and shalt believe in thine heart that God hath raised him from the dead, thou shalt be saved."

Romans 10:10: "For with the heart man believeth unto righteousness; and with the mouth confession is made unto salvation."

Our hearts hold secrets. First Corinthians 14:25 says, "And thus are the secrets of his heart made manifest; and so falling down on his face he will worship God, and report that God is in you of a truth. He has hidden treasures there for us, not from us but from the enemy." Isaiah 45:3 says, "And I will give thee the treasures of darkness, and hidden riches of secret places, that thou mayest know that I, the LORD, which call thee by thy name, am the God of Israel."

Proverbs 4:23 says to guard our hearts: "Keep and "*guard your heart*" with all vigilance and above all that you guard, for *out of it flow the springs of life*." Water is the spiritual representation of the word of God which He wants to reveal to us so we will use it as a weapon against our enemy. Springs of life come from our Lord and Creator. If we didn't have an enemy that wanted our hearts, we wouldn't have been told to guard and pay strict attention to what is happening to the condition of our hearts. Our enemy will come to the mind in our head every time with words he has taken from the Lord, distorting and twisting them into a lie to bring doubt and unbelief to our hearts.

When God speaks to us through the Holy Spirit, it is coming from the throne room of our temple—our heart. God makes our heart open to receive what He wants us to know, if we allow Him. He has planted treasures there not to keep from us but for us to discover. Acts 16:14 says, "And a certain woman named Lydia, a seller of purple, of the city of Thyatira, which worshiped God, heard us: *whose heart the Lord opened*, that she attended unto the things which were spoken of Paul." He also enlarges the capacity of our hearts: "O ye Corinthians, our mouth is open unto you, our *heart* is enlarged" (2 Corinthians 6:11).

God intended for us to have congruency between our heart and mind. If this was not so, He would not have told us about both of them having the ability to have thoughts. Hebrews 8:10 says, "For this is the covenant that I will make with the house of Israel after those days, saith the Lord; I will put my laws (teachings) into their mind, and write them in their hearts: and I will be to them a God, and they shall be to me a people." Hebrews 10:16 says the same thing in reverse to make it known that each have the same thought capabilities, "This is the covenant that I will make with them after those days, saith the Lord, I will put my laws (teachings) into their hearts, and in their minds will I write them." He intends for them to be congruent with each other.

Both the heart's brain and the mind's brain interact with each other either with congruency or incongruency. The results are what show up in our lives.

Chapter 11

Thoughts Originate from Two Energy Systems

God created us with a body, soul and spirit. The world system does not deal with the spirit because it sees things very mechanically and chemically. It focuses largely on the body only. The world system is under the control of Satan, with agreement from man. The world system's approach is basically: spirit represents the nonmaterial spiritual realm and matter represents the material physical realm. The nonmaterial spiritual realm is invisible and not always explainable; therefore science doesn't like it when it can't find hard, logical consistent evidence for what something is and why it is where it is and how it operates.

Humans are looked at as physical matter with mechanical working parts that function because of chemicals and nerve impulses (when they work properly). So when we have a problem, we get a diagnosis from that mindset, based solely upon the set of symptoms we are experiencing. Data from a worldwide database reveals that in the majority of people who share the same set of symptoms, this part or the operating system of the body was the cause for the malfunction. So this chemical should stimulate or shock that area to function appropriately. But at the same time it shocks this area it may also affect several other areas.

This is how they develop drugs and why they have side effects they cannot control. If chemicals don't fix the problem to make something work well enough over time, surgery to extract that malfunctioning part is recommended. So in essence, we are a mechanical machine. The medical community is trained from this thinking. Drugs are developed from this thinking as well.

Methods within the world system have ways to "manage" the mind and body. Science fails to consider that all the connecting answers are found in the spirit connection to the soul and to the Spirit of God. The invisible spirit realm is all the energy in and around us. To not consider the role that spirit plays in our lives is like saying I have no thoughts, feelings, or emotions that cause anything to happen within me. Thoughts, feelings, and emotions are invisible spiritual energies that aren't material. So why do we keep turning to a world system that deals with only two thirds of what we are?

To ignore the spiritual part of us is to ignore all the driving energies from thought and emotions that are causing our physical material to be affected or infected. After all, thoughts and emotions are invisible, not physical or material. It is to say that the spiritual doesn't affect who we are. It is to ignore the realization that there are two invisible spiritual sources that we are fed with food of thought from, every moment of our lives. Energies flow to create positive, healthy operating systems, or weak, negative, toxic operating systems in our body. Then it spreads out into the environment around us.

The greatest disconnect we are making is between us and the God who created us. The world system basically thinks that we don't need God's natures operating in us to give us health and well-being. When we don't consider the role our spirit plays in us, we lack the knowledge of what our spirit needs from God's natures to engage our positive operating system.

God is spirit and He puts part of His spirit in us. We spend more time training, educating, or paying attention to our bodies and minds than we do for our spirit. When it comes to our spiritual immune system, we lack knowledge and remain ignorant. Hosea 4:6 says, "My people are destroyed for lack of knowledge: because thou hast rejected knowledge, I will also reject thee, that thou shalt be no priest to me." We have been deceived just like Adam and Eve.

By now you should have a much better understanding of how your thoughts have everything to do with how you end up with lack of balance and suffer slow death inside of you.

There are Two "Kingdoms of Thought." One is the Kingdom of God and the Other is the Kingdom of Sin.

How do you know where your thoughts are coming from? Positive thoughts create or awaken positive emotional natures within you and originate from God. They are full of light and life. Negative thoughts equal negative emotional states, originating from Satan and his sin kingdom, and are full of death and destruction. They are God's energy distorted by the devil.

The Key is Who You Hook Up With

Strongholds are deep-rooted natures (emotions) within us that come from the kingdom of sin to produce death to your internal trees, to destroy your mind, and to travel to your heart to affect it and hold you captive under bondage and heaviness. God, by the Holy Spirit, comes to build within you mighty trees of righteousness, in exchange for the spirit of heaviness. Isaiah 61:3 says, "To appoint unto them that mourn in Zion, to give unto them beauty for ashes, the oil of joy for mourning, the garment of praise for the spirit of heaviness; that they might be called trees of righteousness, the planting of the LORD, that he might be glorified." Man is compared to trees in many scriptures.

Is it any wonder why God writes in His word about two trees in the Garden of Eden? Think of these two trees representing two types of thoughts that men could potentially listen to. One was a tree of thought in the center of the garden which was a source of all life, it being the ultimate tree of thought coming from God. He was giving Adam a prophetic picture of what He wanted him to know about the evil one (Satan) and to warn him, because he knew Satan would come to man to steal his dominion of authority over the earth. He knew Satan was going to come to man in his thoughts and speak words to him that were twisted from what God had truly said.

So God took Adam to this garden of thought, this garden of knowledge, to tell him that the tree of thought was good for producing and multiplying life. But there was one tree of thought that would not produce a single bit of fruit; the tree of the knowledge of good and evil mixed. One tree stood as man full of the life of God and the other tree stood as a man full of both the life of God and death from evil. In the center of the garden of thoughts was the tree full of all life which represents God.

Tree of Both Good and Evil

This leaves us to understand that there are two "kingdoms of thought." One is the Kingdom of God and the other is the kingdom of sin. These kingdoms are in our mind and will illustrate our thoughts and what we become on earth. It all depends on which tree or kingdom we choose to believe. Genesis 2:9 says, "And out of the ground made the LORD God to grow every tree that is pleasant to the sight, and good for food; the tree of life also in the midst of the garden, and the tree of knowledge of good and evil."

God told Adam not to eat of the fruit of the tree of both good and evil. Genesis 2:17 says, "But of the tree of the knowledge of good and evil, thou shalt not eat of it: for in the day that thou eatest thereof thou shalt surely die." God was warning Adam, telling him in verse 16 that all trees of thought were good to eat from and be nourished, except the one tree of thoughts of good and evil. Why good and evil? Satan takes the word of God which is good and distorts its true meaning to twist it into a lie, for evil.

The devil doesn't have any new curriculum of knowledge to teach, that is why he uses the Word as his knowledge base, to change its true meaning. We have the authority and right to sue him for copyright infringement, provided we know what the original legal document says. He really is as dumb as a box a rocks if we have the understanding of God's word and open our mouth to use it against him. This is why the Bible says in Isaiah, "NO Weapon formed against you shall prosper" (Isaiah 54:17 KJV). It cannot prosper when put up against the word of God coming from inside you.

These trees are in our minds and require us to choose life or death thoughts. Thoughts grow branches that turn into mighty oaks, with thoughts of our true identity as created by God, or which diminish them as if a forest fire of thoughts from the sin kingdom went through our brain.

By the act of our free will, we have the choice to eat and digest thoughts of life and peace, or thoughts of death and destruction, just as Adam and Eve did. Just as food is vital for the energy and nourishment of our physical bodies, so thoughts are the nutritional energy for our entire well-being. Depending on which choice we make, we all grow trees full of life and bear fruit in our brain, or we cause branches to die and bear no fruit.

Mark 7:6 says, "He answered and said unto them, Well hath Esaias prophesied of you hypocrites, as it is written, This people honoureth me with their lips, but their heart is far from me."

Consciousness is Co-perception

The fall made man *self*-conscious. Before the fall, man was only God conscious because his spiritual sight was dominant over his natural sight. He was one with Him in spiritual perception. What God perceived is what man perceived, that is, as much as God intended Adam to know. Not that man was equal to God Himself but man was given, through being in the image of God, as much ability as God created him to have. All with which Adam was created lived and moved in sync with God without effort because they were one with each other. Consciousness is co-perception. Man and God had one perception to their thinking, being one in spirit. Accurate perception is to see beyond the visible; to identify something by means of the five senses and the eyes of the spirit.

The way Adam and Eve had to perceive their world changed after the fall because the spirit of man died in him. It no longer was united to God's spirit because sin entered man and there is no sin in God. So Adam and Eve became detached from God. They lost their spiritual sight of perception and their physical sight was opened instead to physical self- awareness. The world that became open for them to see was the physical world of self which they had never known before they swallowed the wrong thought from the serpent Satan. They became openly aware of themselves. Their dominant way to perceive shifted from the spirit world to the visual sight of the "self"-conscious physical world. This limited them to perceiving themselves and their surroundings through only their five physical senses. This must have been a major jolt to their entire system. They had not learned to communicate and operate like this at all.

When their eyes were opened to this self-conscious world, man saw weaknesses in himself that was never part of him when he knew no sin. He saw that he was naked, not just outside himself, but inside too. Adam and Eve opened themselves up to a foreign world they couldn't understand. It was totally foreign to them. They saw the weaknesses in them and saw themselves naked, as never before. They were seeing themselves like Satan saw. Man knew no sin until he saw and mingled with evil. They were clueless as to how to live life at first.

Today, because of Jesus death on the cross, the Holy Spirit living inside of us is what connects our spirit with God's Spirit, but it is still different than what Adam and Eve had with God before they sinned. We now have to take control of our self-conscious, to keep from building up our "self" too much and choose by an act of our free will to subdue the tree of evil thoughts that still want to grow inside of us.

How we perceive anything, whether it be spiritual or physical, comes from stored emotional beliefs inside of us. Emotions are physical natures expressing themselves through actions known as attitudes. Man had only God's natures, or emotions, capable of being expressed. He only had an operating system that was of positive nature, no negative nature was created in man. Adam had only God's emotional natures and no evil was a part of his spirit man because he was without sin.

Man was originally created without sin, having no knowledge of evil. Man shared the same natures of thought as God, being one in spirit. Adam's spirit perceived what God's expressed natures and characteristics were because he was full of no other emotions but godly ones. He had simple, childlike knowledge to express God's love in its fullness, in flawless purity. He knew how God felt about things because he shared and expressed the same natures with Him.

There energy comingled as one. This gave Adam the ability to name all the animals, thus identifying their intended nature as God had created it within each of them. There was a Spirit to spirit "knowing" between God and Adam.

After the fall all mankind lost this spirit union with God and we have struggled to perceive and know Him in a way He didn't intend for us to learn. This is why we no longer have a true concept of God's love. The love of God is shed abroad in our hearts. Romans 5:5 says, "And hope maketh not ashamed; because the love of God is shed abroad in our hearts by the Holy Ghost which is given unto us."

The seeds of our identity which God planted in our hearts is what Satan seeks to destroy. This is why Matt 13:19 tells us, "When any one heareth the word of the kingdom, and understandeth it not, then cometh the wicked one, and catcheth away that which was sown in his heart."

Zechariah 8:12 says, "For the seed shall be prosperous; the vine shall give her fruit, and the ground shall give her increase, and the heavens shall give their dew; and *I will cause the remnant of this people to possess all these things.*" We have a very big inheritance.

What used to be automatic between God and man's spirit, because of complete union of two spirits, now must be known and understood as we seek Him. This is spoken of in Luke 12:31 and Matthew 6:33 which says, "But seek ye first the kingdom of God, and his righteousness; and all these things shall be added unto you." Where is the Kingdom of God? It is inside of you when you become born again and your spirit is made new. Matthew 13:19 tells us that it is in our heart: "When any one heareth the word of the kingdom, and understandeth it not, then cometh the wicked one, and catcheth away that which was sown in his heart."

Communication with God

This is why communication with God is impaired. We now have to be Holy Spirit directed into the knowledge of God's love for us. This involves engaging of our heart with God's love. Second Thessalonians 3:5 says, "And the Lord direct your hearts into the love of God." Man wants to wall up his heart to avoid being hurt.

Second Corinthians 9:7 says, "Every man according as he purposeth in his heart."

By default we try to understand God's love by the measuring stick of the world. There are two kingdoms: one a kingdom of the world and one a kingdom of God which is of Spirit. There is no comparison or definition of love that equals the definition of love from God's perception.

We now automatically view everything self-consciously coming from our mind and battle with what the Spirit in our heart wants to tell us is the true perception. This is because we have been negatively programmed against the truth our entire life. From the truth is how we should form our beliefs, so our perceptions aren't wrong. The truth is found in the word of God.

This has strongly affected us and who we become everyday, because of the way we have learned and been programmed to believe certain things. Those beliefs, right or wrong, are the lens we use to give meaning and perception to what we see. This is why Satan distorts our self-conscious to make us more aware of ourselves and less aware of the truth about the God who created us. The more you see with your natural senses, the less you see with the eyes of your spirit. The eyes of the spirit must be developed.

When man sinned, our spirit connection of unity with God died. A veil went up, separating the unity of co-perception man had with God in one united spirit consciousness.

Why? Because Satan knew that there is no sin within God, nor can sin co-exist in unity with God. Therefore, he knew that if he could get man to curse himself, man would curse God and cause a separation between man and God. After all, this is what happened between Satan and God. He duplicates what he did in himself, and in one third of the angels, thinking in the thoughts of mankind.

He knew that if he could influence man's "self"-conscious to agree with his thoughts, he would get possession of earth back, which he lost when God judged the iniquity found in his heart. By getting man to curse himself, he would be able to corrupt the seed that was planted on earth when God created man from earth. He would also thwart the multiplication of God's bride. I believe Satan wanted to be the bride, the fourth part of the Godhead. The bride could create and was in God's likeness and image. Satan can't create; he can only re-create to destroy. This makes him possessed with envy.

Satan lost a lot of frequencies of God energy to change the earth and influence nations on the earth with his agenda. He wanted it all back, to possess the earth and earth's inhabitants. He lost his voice of dominion in the earth. Satan trained one third of the angels that fell with him to have a voice and dominion in the earth for evil.

Don't you think some of those angels ruled nations on the earth before Adam? Don't you think Satan had ultimate rulership over the earth at that time? What good is a being without a voice to influence and speak with authority and power to dictate orders in the earth? They all lost their voices on the earth when they chose to rebel against God.

Satan needed his voice to be heard in the earth, and the way he did that was to cause man to fall just as he had, to open the access point for him to "speak" through man and rule on the earth once again. So he waited and watched for the right moment to steal the dominion over earth from man, so he could put his voice back in the earth legally, to control and dominate it once again. He wasn't about to stand by and watch man take over that over which he once had rulership. Nor was he about to allow the bride of Christ to multiply earth with more of God's glory and presence. He wanted to be worshiped by all of God's creation and for things to be put under his rule, just as before. Only this time he wanted to be god over everything God had created and to be worshiped with all the glory of God. He thinks he can take God's place. He said he was higher than God.

Chapter 12

Guard your Heart

Neuroscientists tell us that our emotional center is actually the non-conscious or the limbic section of our brain. We have talked about the brain of the heart influencing the conduct of the brain in our head. Our emotional natures reside in our heart, which is the throne room for the Holy Spirit and our spirit. Since our spiritual heart is the center of our being and the wellspring for whom we are, Proverbs 4:23 tells us, "Keep thy heart with all diligence; for out of it are the issues of life." Psalm 119:11 adds, "Your word have I laid up in my heart, that I might not sin against You" (AMP).

Satan knew that he was going to have to change the condition of the heart between man and God. He went through the mind of man to do it. Entering deceptive thoughts into the mind of man is the connection to corrupt man's heart. Once the heart of man begins to be corrupted, he knew he had for himself mouth pieces to speak in the earth.

Matthew 15:18-20 says, "But those things which proceed out of the mouth come forth from the heart; and they defile the man. For out of the heart proceed evil thoughts, murders, adulteries, fornications, thefts, false witness, blasphemies: These are the things which defile a man: but to eat with unwashen hands defileth not a man." If we ever thought words didn't matter, this verse shows how wrong we were. Our "words," or our "Words," have all to do with it! Our words can become Satan's words or they can become

God's "Words." We hold the creative powers, therefore our words do create stuff.

Do you realize that you are capable of creating? Do you realize that you are creating all the time?

This may well challenge your thinking. What is really happening here on earth that has to do with God and us? Allow the Holy Spirit to speak to you spirit to spirit, while you read the next group of thoughts. Listen to your heart to hear what your head might silence.

Our Future "is" Our Present Speaking

In your present you are choosing what energy force you are tapping into to create your life. This will be energy from the light of God or the darkness of the enemy to create what could be your life and physical state. We are limitless, always exuding energy that is co-mingling with like energy. The question is what are we co-mingled with more of the time, positive or negative?

Matthew 16:19 says, "And I will give unto thee the keys of the kingdom of heaven: and whatsoever thou shalt bind on earth shall be bound in heaven: and whatsoever thou shalt loose on earth shall be loosed in heaven."

Nothing that we propose to do can be withheld. How many of you think there is a future "out there" waiting to happen for you? How many believe that the future is fate, that we really don't have a say about what will happen in the future? What if I suggested to you that there really is no future *"out there"*? We live in a space of time with possibilities and those possibilities are in our present space. We don't move into a future because our future is in our present. *Everything possible is sitting in our present with us now, as possibilities through thoughts and how we perceive.* Matthew 19: 26 says, "But Jesus beheld them, and said unto them, With men this is impossible; but with God all things are possible."

But what seems possible is way beyond our ability to imagine. Isaiah 55:9 says, "For as the heavens are higher than the earth, so are my ways higher than your ways, and my thoughts than your thoughts." Our conscious mind limits us to think that is a factual statement. Rather, we could perceive it to be something to move into by the act of asking Him. After all, does He not speak of a desire in Him, of wanting to give us the things that are hidden? Isaiah 45:3 says, "And I will give you the treasures of darkness and hidden riches of secret places, that you may know that it is I, the Lord, the God of Israel, Who calls you."

Our limits to possibilities are not a problem, our problem is that we aren't aware that possibilities existence in nature. Being aware is accurate perception. The *mistake we make is to live, believing our future happens as if we have no say about it.* That is false perception.

May I be allowed to speak the truth, and you be open to hear it? We "say" everything about "life" because the future exists *"in our speaking"*. To the degree you speak unknowingly, your past is speaking who you are, we can't create our future, but are repeating our past, and will be kept tied to it by this very "thought." It keeps you super-glued to your past.

The darkest blindness of all is to never gain the knowledge that your future is created by your speaking and your actions, which come from the "thoughts you dwell upon."

Hebrews 11:1: "Now faith is the substance of things hoped for, the evidence of things not seen."

Romans 10:17: "So then faith cometh by hearing, and hearing by the word of God."

James 2:26: "For as the body without the spirit is dead, so faith without works is dead also."

James 3:8: "But the tongue can no man tame; it is an unruly evil, full of deadly poison."

We create our future with behaviors stuck on auto pilot and we are oblivious that we do it. To know this is to realize that every "thought" increases possibilities. Your "present" holds each word and each action for your future. By what means does it? Your thoughts and how you build your thinking to speak your heart.

Now does that mean you can just speak and it will be? Not exactly! It is the relationships that you connect with that will provide the space for possibilities. Connecting with your Creator God will create a fit to the whole picture as He is the only one who creates the beginning from the end. Ecclesiastes 3:11 says, "He hath made every thing beautiful in his time: also he hath set the world in their heart, so that no man can find out the work that God maketh from the beginning to the end."

With each act of obedience which you fit into the whole, the possibilities increase. Possibilities to comprehend are beyond our imaginations, but they are not altogether impossible. Isaiah 55:9 says, "For as the heavens are higher than the earth, so are my ways higher than your ways, and my thoughts than your thoughts." Matthew 19:26 says, " But Jesus beheld them, and said unto them, With men this is impossible; but with God all things are possible"

With more possibilities that manifest, more room or space is created. That is God's law of producing multiplication. But to the degree that the past is repeated, we shrink space for possibilities. Choices are set in stone, based upon taking captive every thought in our present.

God Forgets our Repented Sins

God doesn't remember our sins. The blood changes that stain in you and removes it. We act to remember, it requires an action inside of us to remember. God has no memory of our sin once we repent from it. How do you remember something you don't remember? Have you ever tried to remember something that someone else said you did, and you can't remember doing it, no matter how hard you try? That is what God does with your sin—it is impossible for Him to remember.

How can God, who *knows no sin*, remember what He doesn't know? In other words, God doesn't have any frequencies of energy to His being that are sin distorted frequencies, therefore how can He have a memory of that which never resonates within Him? It is impossible for Him to remember your sin that has been washed clean by the blood of Jesus. There is newly formed energy that canceled out the old.

To remember requires a harmony of the energy that was involved with that event. When you remember, you resonate or call up the same set of energies that were involved when the event took place. This is what happens when you recall a memory. Why would He make a choice to be in harmony with your sin's energies from the recall of a sin event? Why would He resonate with any of sin's energy? He cannot, for sin is not within Him.

We are the ones who can choose to resonate with energies and the nature of those frequencies, or vibrations, because we can choose to be part of the world's evil energy, or choose to not be of the world. We can believe that the memory of sin is gone.

We move God when, with our faith, we resonate with what He has told us, either by a revelation we receive or by claiming any of the promises from His word. Why is that so important? When we agree and believe what He has said to us, we are transmitting those frequencies of thoughts. When we transmit those same vibrations of energy in thought and speak them back to God, we double the power of the energy wave.

Remember our previous illustration of the wave? When one wave joins another wave of the same energy frequencies, it doubles in strength. This is how we move God by the working of our faith. What is faith? The substance of things hoped for but the evidence of things not seen.

This is illustrated in the physical, for example, when the woman with the issue of blood touched Jesus in Matthew 9:20, "And, behold, a woman, which was diseased with an issue of blood twelve years, came behind him, and touched the hem of his garment:" The original translation actually says that "someone tapped into me." It was her energy of faith to connect and be in harmony with Jesus' energy that brought about her miracle by altering her distorted energy which had produced the problems in her blood.

The woman tapped into Jesus' perfect set of energetic frequencies, causing her distorted vibrations to conform into the perfect wave forms of Jesus. She received her miracle by the action of faith, the action of having hope in the invisible. She put her faith into operation. You could say you work your thoughts of energy by telling yourself and making a heart connection to conform to what you believe Jesus already possesses. He has all of your healings or miracles of divine energy because He holds all things together. She speaks what she believes in her heart in Matthew 9:21-22 "For she said within herself, If I may but touch his garment, I shall be whole. But Jesus turned him about, and when he saw her, he said, Daughter, be of good comfort; thy faith hath made thee whole. And the woman was made whole from that hour."

This is why it is so important to not allow your heart to harden. When you harden your heart you are saying with your logical physical mind, "Unless I see it, I won't believe it." This is you erecting a "Do not enter!" sign on your heart. You need your heart to connect, to tap into and ride the wave of God's energies to become harmonious with those vibrations of energy that cause positive changes of healing or miracles. If you harden your heart, what you pray for can't happen. You don't hear the word of God, nor do you speak it out. You block your ability to receive the frequencies, the energies of God.

His word and revelation that He gives you must be spoken out of you. Light from God must be put off by you, by speaking. Revelation comes to you in your heart and the Word is light. The heart is the throne room of the Holy Spirit; the Holy Spirit is the messenger of the Word to you.

Photons are packets of light, so when those thoughts/ photons enter you, a negative electron is released from you. Revelation is the word of God, the light of God, the energy of God coming into you, and once in you, they must be spoken out to have any manifestation. God spoke everything into existence and so must we. Light holds the set of frequencies that cause manifestations from heaven to earth. Ask God to reveal what you should speak. Speak what you hear from Him, for this is the way you create.

Man is made in God's image and likeness. He told man to multiply in the earth, but that doesn't just mean to have babies. Stay in harmony with God. Don't doubt or allow the enemy to steal your light. Stay in harmony, in tune by faith for what you are believing for. You find out what to believe by personal revelation that He gives to your heart or by claiming for yourself the promises in His word.

Chapter 13

It Isn't In Your Genes.

You may feel that all of this is well and good, but that you can't help the way you are because you are the way you are because of the genes you were born with. That is based on outdated science. It has been discovered that you are not the way you are because of genes. This knowledge is very freeing because you now have the freedom to know that you have the power to change who you are, both physically and mentally. You don't have to wait for that same sickness to capture you that your parent died from. That is good news.

But you might ask why it seems to be true. Some may say both their parents died of cancer or a heart attack. Why is that if it isn't in the genes? Realize what you have been taught about thoughts already to answer how it is happening. You can't call God a liar. His Word says, "As a man thinketh, so is he."

Let's explain where this belief that "we are who we are because of our genes," came from and why this continues to be brought forth as truth when it is error. Many scientists discovered this up to twenty years ago now! One of the easiest books to understand in laymen's language about this is *The Biology of Belief*, written by Bruce Lipton, a scientist.

Cell Biology 101

Scientists assumed that the genes in our DNA were the "brain" of our cells. They were found in the nucleus of a cell. The brain is defined as, "the organ responsible for controlling and coordinating the physiology and behaviors of any organism." Or simply put, according to the medical model, "the human body is a biochemical machine that the genes control, and the brain is secondary to the genes." According to this thinking, whatever we are born with in the genes, we are controlled by them. That is another way of saying that the mind is just in the brain's imagination, inside a machine of physical matter.

They assumed that the nucleus of a cell contained the brain of a cell, which also has the DNA material. So that meant when you removed the nucleus of the cell, it should result in the cell dying. By assuming this to be fact, they never questioned if the nucleus was in fact the cell's brain.

So the scientists took the cell into the OR (operating room) to do surgery, performing a procedure called enucleation. In this procedure, the scientist takes a needle and sticks it into the cell's cytoplasmic interior. He calls for suction and the nucleus is sucked out of the cell's center. In the needle is the cell's brain ripped out. The cell should be dead without a brain.

What they saw next was a moment of: "Houston, we have a problem." The cell never stopped moving—it was still as alive as ever. The wound from the needle closed, and like anyone after surgery; it staggered about a little, but soon got to its feet. (Only subsequently it "ran away" from its surgeon with the needle. Cells aren't stupid.)

In fact, what they found out is, cells with their nuclei sucked out can survive up to two months or more without their genes. They don't lie around, nor do they need life support administered. They continue to live and perform the day to day functions of digestion, respiration, excretion, metabolization, and so on. They are able to grow and respond correctly when needing protection from their environment. They are able to communicate with other cells. Looking back, scientists should have known that genes couldn't provide the control for our lives.

What they did find out, was that genes are responsible for cells being able to divide and reproduce their parts. This inability results in dysfunctions due to defective proteins which eventually lead to the cell's death. *Cells without their nucleus don't die because they lost their brain but because they lost their ability to reproduce their worn or torn parts.* So you could say that the nucleus of *the cell is the gonad, the reproductive part.*

With the nucleus of the cell stripped out, without death as a result, it implies that the cell's "brain" is still operating and intact. This is shown by the fact that the cells keep their biological functions without having any genes.

We will read a little later about where the genome project came from, but for now let's look at what they did discover, which blew their assumptions out of the water. This new science is called "epigenetics." "Epi" in Greek means "above or over." This science revealed that life is controlled by something above the genes. What scientists found has shaken Biology to its very core, largely because it reveals that we aren't victims, we are masters of our genes. It proved our role in life is to be able to co-create our reality.

Genes Aren't our Destiny

As it turns out, the membrane or skin of cells reads environmental signals and regulates the gene's activities. This makes us the master over our genes and not the other way around. Genes aren't our destiny! This is what they discovered:

Our cells, all fifty plus trillion or so of them, have a population of proteins that make up their membranes, their skin. These proteins are divided into two groups: receivers and transmitters. The receivers are called "receptors," while transmitters are called "effectors." The receptors take in information from the cells exterior while the effectors take that information into the cell's nucleus.

Receptors look like antennas that read vibrational energy fields like sound, air wave frequencies, and light. They read fields of energy from the environment. These receptors are energy antennas that vibrate like a tuning fork. When an energy vibration resonates from the environment with the receptor's antenna, it will alter the charge of the protein, causing it to change its shape. When the receptor (receiver) provides a signal, then there has to be a life sustaining response on the part of the cell that is generated.

When the electrical charge on the receptor protein is altered, its shape change creates an opening. The effector (transmitter) then makes an effect, sending a signal to the interior or nucleus of the cell. This activates any of the functions of the cell that are required for the cell to live. The effector can change the respiration rate of the cell or any other behaviors of the cell, like digestion, or movement.

This action turns your cells into a biological battery which is recharged continually. Some of these functions throw more positive charges into the cell than are let out by the cell. At times, cells can have positive charges on the inside and negative charges on the outside (or vice versa).

You know this by how your body regulates temperature, for example. If you step outside and find it is hot, your cells read that signal, internalizing the information to your body to keep your temperature at 98.6 degrees. You have certain receptors for temperature information and different ones for estrogen, calcium, glucose, histamine, and any of the hormones or stress factors. There are receptors for every function needed for the body to sustain life.

The skin of your body and the skin of a single cell are doing the exact same thing. They read signals from the environment and engage an effect to the nucleus of the cell, so it stays in balance. The eyes in your head are not the only things that take in light. Your ears are not the only thing on our body that takes in sound. All of the cells of the skin, for example, have receptors to identify the signals from light and sound. That is why we can have our eyes closed and the cells on our skin still know that it is light or dark, which is why people in Alaska, (where there are extended periods of light and darkness) have greater problems with moods.

Just like when the skin of our human body reads a signal, the signal is sent to the interior of the body. Then the physiology of the body is adjusted to meet the need shown to it from the environment. This same thing happens in the cells on the inside of the body, the receptors read the environment, and an activated receptor will change its electrical charge, change shape, and will then couple with an effector protein. Then an electrical signal is sent into the cell to cause a specific function.

The signal will either tell the functions of that cell to move towards the signal or away from the signal. So when no signal is present, the effector isn't engaged and won't control the function. We could call these "electrical switches." They turn things on or off in the cell. The membrane's receptors are like sensory nerves, and the effectors are like motor nerves that generate movement or actions.

These electrical switches are built into the membrane of the cell. When working properly and reading signals properly, they will engage necessary biological functions of the body. On the surface of any one cell there are over one hundred thousand switches for one hundred thousand electrical impulses. If you want to know what every one of them is doing at any moment in time, it is impossible to track.

The bottom line is that every switch functions the same. In the membrane, there is a switch designed to read the signal from the environment, to then find a connection with an effector protein. The effector protein will cause an internal function that will meet the demand called for from the environment. Through this continual adjusting of our internal operational needs, we can move from one environment to another and our cells will automatically read and reread, adjust and readjust to the ever-changing stimuli that are presented in any given moment. It is the integration of all these functions that collectively cause our behavior to become what it is, from our past to present.

Do your cells need more adrenalin, testosterone, or calcium? How does the receptor switch find the effector switch to provide the cell with these? Like energy attracts like energy. The frequency of energy for adrenaline, testosterone, or calcium is read and supplied.

So the switch is made up of two components of protein, the receptor (receiver) and the effector (transmitter). The switch is the "interconnection" between the environments outside of the cell, and the response created inside the cell (in the nucleus). It is important to realize then that the switch is the absolute thing that will cause the behavior from the cell. This is going to happen based upon the perception of the cell's receptor.

Stimulus from the environment is picked up by the receiver (receptor) and the response will be a manifestation from the output of the transmitter (effector). Cells are a stimulus response device that controls the function of the cell. Now because the function of the membrane is this, it performs as a brain for the cell membrane of fifty plus trillion cells that make up the body. The membranes of the cells are working brains because these switches read the environment, control the functions and unite or incorporate the behavior on the inside of the cells.

For a cell to have intelligence, it must have a membrane with functional receptors for awareness and effectors for actions. The ability for the membrane of the cell to interact with the environment with intelligence, to produce behaviors, is what makes it the "brain" of the cell. Information is perceived and sent across this vast domain of trillions of cells through these hundred thousand switches on each cell. This operation controls the functions of our lives.

Summary

In summary, the energetic switches that control life are the receptors that read awareness of the environment and the transmitter (effector) conveys a message by a physical sensation that controls the moving parts. The operation of each individual cell and all cells throughout the body operate the same. That operation is the definition of perception.

"Perception" is defined as "a single unified awareness derived from sensory processes while a stimulus is present." It is being aware of the physical environment via a physical sensation. Protein switches read perceptions and then make biological adjustments to fit the perceptions. The way we perceive controls our behavior.

A function is generated by proteins to create a certain behavior. The behavior is generated by a signal. The signal comes from the cell membrane to the center of the cell via the perception switch. The perception switch is engaged from an environmental stimulus. The behavioral actions of our cells are originally caused by the signals from the environment. This makes the behavior of an organism the direct reflection of what is in the environment and how that organism perceives its environment.

Perception controls behavior. This means that if the perceptions are accurate, the biological balances will be good, but if we have been programmed with misperceptions and read our environment inaccurately, it will result in wrong responses and can cause our operating systems to become dysfunctional or diseased.

So where did the genes go? They have to do something. What do they do? They are in the cell (as we found out when they got sucked out and the cell continued to live). If they don't control their own activity or our behavior, as originally thought, what do they do?

Remember our effectors (transmitters) that give off electrical signals to create an action or behavior from the cell? It turns out that their signals activate genes. The effector proteins control the reading of the genes so that worn out proteins get replaced and new proteins can be created. They are stored blueprints. Remarkably, the genetic information of our DNA holds blueprints that get chosen based upon what our perception of our environment is at any moment. The environment is controlling the read out of the genes by the switches on the skin of the cells.

Cell Switches are Perception

We have called these switches perception. Perception controls both the behavior of the cell and the reading of the genes. And based off of our perception, we are going to select a blueprint with a genetic readout to it. That will control the mechanism to make a provision for our lives, either a correct one for balancing us or one of error that will cause a dysfunction in the cell. (You can actually divert the biology of the cell and cause dysfunction and disease in the cell.) When enough of these misperceptions cause in-accurate biological functions to accumulate across a vast number of cells, the body develops these dysfunctions or diseases.

We play the role of a powerful contractor that does the selecting of blueprints, based upon our perceived realities, plus signals and stimuli from our environment.

For those who are reading this who have deeper knowledge of all this, I feel I need to include this information. There is one period of time during development when the genes play a greater role over the role of perception, and that is after conception. There is a period of time after conception when the embryo grows enough to be considered a fetus. During this time the genes are mapping and feeding information to this tiny life. But once the baby is a fetus, then all of the perceptions from the mother are downloaded to the baby via the blood, through the umbilical cord.

For ninety-five percent of us, there are no birth defects as a result of mutated genes. Ninety-five percent of the population is born with healthy sets of genes. The other five percent can be negatively impacted in life by the genes they carry and can be born with birth defects. But the vast majority is not impacted negatively during the time of the babies' growth where there is more gene control. The ninety-five percent of those born will be born with information that was downloaded as a result of how the mother perceived the environment and what was happening to her. When a baby is born, the parts of that baby that are weaker or stronger is based upon the perceptions carried inside to the baby through the mother.

You may say if this is true, then why do they still try to tell us that our disease or our bodies' dysfunctions are due to our genes? Bruce Lipton explains it this way in his book *The Biology of Belief*:

> In 1990, under the direction of James Watson, with the interests of the U.S. National Institute of Health (NIH), and an agency of the U.S. Department ODF Health and Human Services, the Human Genome Project (HGP) was birthed. This project had three main objectives which were to create a research database with tools to analyze the data that would be shared with bio-technical industries and the private sector; to identify positive and negative human traits from a genetic base; and to promote and develop new medical applications around the globe.

This sounds good, so what does it really mean? Their thinking was based on faulty assumptions that genes controlled an organism's traits. (It was bad science to assume anything before it was proven.) Science doesn't start with an assumption and try to find the elements to fit their presumed hypothesis. That is one of their research rules.

They set out to find one hundred thousand proteins in the human body. With a gene blueprint needed to make each protein, they assumed there should be at least that many genes. Those behind the project set out to make a list, or inventory of all human genes. They could then use that database to engineer a human utopia.

There were other ulterior motives for this project as well. Genetic scientists convinced venture capitalists that a fortune could be made once they identified all one hundred thousand genes. They could patent the nucleotide base sequence for each gene and then sell the information to drug companies who would use them to discover more drugs, make bigger profits and get investors a higher return.

Instead of what they hoped to discover, they found:

The assumption that more complex organisms would possess a greater number of genes (due to more functions involved) was incorrect. They found this out after beginning their study on the genes of the simpler organisms.

Bacteria, the most primitive organism, contain three-thousand to five-thousand genes. The Cenorhabditias elegans, a barely visible round worm made up of 1271 cells had about twenty three thousand genes. So far, the assumptions were not working out.

Next they went to the more complex fruit fly and were surprised in the wrong way. It had only eighteen thousand genes. That begged the question of how a more complex organism can have fewer genes than the simple round worm. (That should have caused them to say, "Houston, we have a problem here.")

When the project was completed and all the results were in, they were staggered by how incorrect their assumptions had been. In other words, if the results of what they were looking for had been intended to solve a problem at NASA, with the lives of astronauts on the line—say to enter the earth's atmosphere without a hitch—they would be planning funerals instead of having a celebration. In the end, the results of their testing revealed that as biologically complex as we humans are, with our fifty plus trillion cells, we have approximately twenty-three thousand genes—about the same number as the barely visible round worm.

Nevertheless, the results of the project were reported in 2003, and spoken of as if it had been one of humanity's greatest accomplishments. Dr. Paul Silverman, a pioneer in the research and a principal architect of the project, responded by saying that science needed to rethink the notion of genetic determinism.

Silverman wrote in the magazine called *The Scientist May 2004*: "The cell signaling process heavily depends on extracellular stimuli to trigger nuclear DNA transduction." Translated: ***It isn't in the genes, it's in the environment.***

I found it fascinating that one gene blueprint can make over two thousand different products. Humans have some twenty three thousand genes. These genes are the building blocks for the human houses you and I create. We are the contractors, choosing which blueprints we read based upon electrical signals of perception from reading our environment.

It is Our Perception

Once we understand the new science of epigenetics and throw out the story telling us that we are victims of our genes, we then realize that the control is in our "perception". This shows the role we have played as a victim is gone and we are free to know that there is nothing that is impossible for us to create if we only change our perception. Yes, our perceptions are so powerful that they can change all the combinations of read-outs in our genes.

There are possibilities that our perceptions hold that are so powerful—if only we would act in faith for those possibilities. Just as there are an infinite number of possibilities that a computer can calculate, so are the possibilities even greater using our God-given "computer."

Once again we come back to this: our thoughts and our beliefs hold enormous power, if our perceptions are right. We are filled with misperceptions as downloaded programs from childhood on. The good news is that these programs can be changed. That is what the Word tells us. It says we are to be transformed by the renewing of our minds. Romans 12:2 says, "And be not conformed to this world: but be ye transformed by the renewing of your mind," Both brains need to be active and congruent, both the brain of our heart and of our head. Mark 9:23 says, "Jesus said unto him, If thou can believe, all things are possible to him that believeth." This is literally true.

Chapter 14

Has Quantum Physics Found God's Energy?

We need to understand how our cells operate to interpret what is going on around us. In order to do that, let us look a little deeper to understand the energy of God which spoke everything into existence. Has quantum physics discovered God's energy in action at the subatomic level of everything's core existence?

We must explore the physics which prove that our perceptions are causing things inside of us "to be" as well as outside of us (in our environment). How does this happen? By the way we "observe"! Remember this: *What we observe, we receive.*

Quantum physics is relevant to biology, as Bruce Lipton and many other scientists discovered. Lipton says that biologists are making a glaring, scientific error by ignoring its laws. Physics, after all, is the foundation of all the sciences, yet biologists want to stick to the outdated Newtonian model that says "all matter is made up of matter," and ignore the invisible quantum world of Einstein, in which all matter is made up of energy and there are no absolutes.

Quantum physics is the study of the smallest quantity of radiant energy. Physics is the study of matter, down to the atom. When physics decided to ask the question of what made up an atom, they discovered something they didn't expect. They didn't find matter inside an atom, they found invisible energy. They found spinning vortices of energy that had positive and negative charges, known as photons and electrons. These vortices, spinning like little tornadoes of energy, are found in everything we see as physical matter, including us. Nothing exists without energy. When you think about it, why wouldn't this be the case? God spoke everything into existence. Everything has the breath of God, the energy of God in its physical makeup.

God gave mankind free will with all possibilities of perception based on choice. The invisible world is the next nanosecond ahead of you. You call that next nanosecond from invisible to visible reality by observing and speaking. Our life is what we perceive and declare from the way we perceive. This sounds just like what God's word tells us, doesn't it? We must be careful what we think about, speak out, and observe in our imagination. We cause it to be!

There is a connected consciousness that we have with God. We receive information faster than the speed of light from the Holy Spirit. This is how prophecies get here that predict the future. Everything is made up of atoms, which are made up of frequencies of energy, spinning very fast. These frequencies are the voice of Jesus because He is the word who spoke everything into existence. He is holding all things together, causing things to be as we physically see them. We could say Jesus sings the frequencies or vibrations of your body, and all of creation. You either resonate with Him, or you resonate with the fallen kingdom.

Your DNA Sings a Unique Song

Did you know there is a song in your DNA? A molecular biologist converted protein sequences into classical music. A chord was assigned to each amino acid. You can listen to a protein. Proteins are what your fifty trillion cells are made of that constitute you! You can listen to your song. For more information go to: http://www.mimg.ucla.edu/faculty/miller_jh/gene2music/examples.html or search the internet for DNA song.

This scripture in Psalm 28:7 is literal. "The LORD is my strength and my shield; my heart trusted in him, and I am helped: therefore my heart greatly rejoiceth; and *with my song will I praise him*. We have a unique song that no one else sings.

You are not a solid object. Man was originally created from dust. Genesis 2:7 says, "And the LORD God formed man of the dust of the ground, and breathed into his nostrils the breath of life; and man became a living soul." God breathed His voice of energetic frequencies into us. Our unique sets of frequencies are what set us apart from one another. We are made up of subatomic structures, particles, and electrons (negative charges of energy). Quantum mechanics has confirmed that the stuff you and I are made up of "blinks" in and out of this reality, or dimension.

Think about what happened to Enoch. Genesis 5:24 says, "By faith Enoch was translated that he should not see death; and was not found, because God had translated him" So how much of the invisible world do we realize is a part of the spiritual realm and in existence here?

David Van Koevering, a physicist, inventor, and musicologist who came to the Lord after dying twelve times, makes quantum physics a bit easier to understand in his books called, *"Keys to Taking your Quantum Leap"* and *"Quantum Healing."* He explains that when you look inside an atom you will find it is made up of subatomic particles. Subatomic particles are made up of superstrings. Superstrings are tiny packets of energy (vortices of energy) that spin at a frequency. (see figure 21.) They are the vibrations at the core of all matter. Jesus is holding all things together that we see in the physical.

Figure 21: Vortices of energy spinning illustrated

Energy is everywhere around us. These packets of energy are not real to our five senses in this dimension because they exist in "possibilities" only, until someone observes them as something. Once someone observes them in their thoughts, these packets of invisible energy become a thing, either a particle or a wave. This is known as the Double Slit Experiment. This experiment proves that "what you perceive, you receive"—you cause it to be. The experiment that made this discovery works like this.

Take a thin sheet of metal that has two slits in it about a quarter of an inch wide and about twelve inches long. Behind the screen is a photosensitive detector that detects photons of light. When you take light and ask a person to observe the light as particles it will appear through the two slits as particles. Particles show up like a shotgun blast—dots all over. Particles are a burst of energy.

For example, if the person is asked to observe the light as waves, using the same light you used previously (or any other kind of light), the person will perceive and observe waves. Waves appear as rings of vibrations or waves. (Like when you drop a stone in a pond and the water forms rings that move outward from where the stone went into the water, see figure 15. & 16.) The light appears as what you called it to be, whether as particles or waves.

Waves or particles make up all matter, including our bodies, which cause that matter to blink into existence when a person observes them in their thoughts. Your thoughts are invisible energy. This process of observation is called "popping a qwiff."

A qwiff is a quantum wave function that collapses upon your observation. This happens to us all the time. Engineers know they will solve a problem if they can pop a qwiff. Whenever you get those aha moments of a solution to a problem, or a divine revelation that you suddenly know that you know something you didn't know before, that is referred to as popping a qwiff.

Everything built, planned, invented or sold required "observing." That sale, that completed building, that completed invention—everything began as an observation in our thought process. Plans start out as unseen, but with your desire, your intent, and with your observation, they become creations and manifest into the seen world within you and around you.

Be careful! You are going to cause a wave (or a particle), with your words in that nanosecond that is coming. This makes it seem foolish to say, "Sticks and stones may break my bones but words will never harm me." You get the point. It will become even clearer as we continue exploring. I hope you see from what I've shown so far that science proves the Word of God to be true. Stick with me and don't miss out on any qwiffs that are coming.

You must understand that when God shows you something that you can't see in the natural yet, He requires action on your part. The action is happening when, what and how you observe things in your world. What is He trying to get you to do? Believe what He is speaking to you, so you can observe what He has shown you. His divine energy must flow through you into this earth realm to make what is seen on the inside of you physical in the earth. He needs you to birth the picture He has revealed to you. Bill Gates and others would not have built the world's largest software business, *Microsoft* had it not been for taking his thoughts into observing the finished working product.

By observing, which is an act of paying attention or focusing on the same thoughts, we create particles or waves. All matter that we see with our senses is made up of particles, or waves. This matter is "blinking" into existence by being observed by a person's thinking. Obviously, this is happening at a rate of speed that we can't see with our natural eyes.

Quantum physicists have discovered that information is exchanged instantly through what they call *"quantum entanglement."* They have found that once two particles touch, they remain interconnected and they cannot be disconnected in the invisible. Einstein referred to this as "spooky action at a distance." You read about this earlier. Your body is made up of photons (light particles) and negatively charged electrons; you can't see them they are so tiny.

All particles, and/or waves seem to be connected to all other particles and waves, which reminds me of what the Word says in First Corinthians 12:12, "For as the body is one, and hath many members, and all the members of that one body, being many, are one body: so also is Christ." Romans 12:5 says, "So we, being many, are one body in Christ, and every one member's one of another." Finally,

First Corinthians 12:20 says, "But now are they many members, yet but one body."

These light particles and waves are blinking in and out of existence because of Jesus. Frequencies are energy, and all frequencies are the voice of Jesus (superstrings). He is the Word. He spoke and it became. He causes all things to be. Colossians 1:16-17 says, "For by Him all things were created that are in heaven and that are on earth, visible and invisible, whether thrones, or dominions, or principalities or powers. All things were created through Him and for Him. And He is before all things, and in Him all things consist." (cohere, are held together). Jesus quit blinking Enoch into this realm. How close do you think Jesus is to you?

We move God when out of our faith we resonate, or harmonize, in like energy with Him and with what He has told us, either by a revelation, or in His word, through His promises. How or why, is that so important? Look again at the wave illustration we viewed earlier. (See figure 14, on page 71.)

When we agree and believe what He has revealed to us, we are transmitting those frequencies of energy in sync and harmony with those thoughts He spoke to us. When we transmit those same energies by agreeing with and meditating on those thoughts, and by speaking them, we double the power of the energy wave.

Remember our illustration of the wave, plus one, minus one when another wave joins that wave of the same energy frequencies, it doubles in vibrational strength and explodes the glass. We move God by the working of our faith. Faith is what? It is the substance (the energy) of things hoped for but the evidence of things not seen. This is why it is impossible to please God without faith. Hebrews 11:6 says, "But without faith it is impossible to please him: for he that cometh to God must believe that he is." We must believe what He has said is true. So true that we can take it to the bank and cash it like a check. (the later chapter on faith will provide more detail)

So what is happening in the invisible realm when we believe? We are in agreement and harmonizing with the same frequencies of thought that speak of something that is for real. Real enough that we can see it in our mind before it even manifests. God created us to create and we do this even without realizing it. Information rides to us on thought waves. Everything starts with thought. Even God thought of how he wanted earth and everything He put into it before He spoke it from His thoughts into existence. He saw it first.

Reconsider from earlier that waves are made more powerful when their frequencies are in harmonic resonance with like frequencies. When waves are in sync with each other, they increase in vibration. When waves are out of sync, not in harmony with each other, the result is destructive interference which *cancels* the original wave or atom vibrations, causing the atom to stop spinning.

Now think about the walls of Jericho coming down. Think about what happened in the upper room. Think about the woman with the issue of blood, tapping into Jesus. It takes energies of belief to connect and be in harmony with Jesus' perfect energy to alter distorted energies—the cause of physical problems. One needs to observe themselves healed and believe from their heart that when they tap into Jesus (divine energy) that is the process of being made whole. The perception of truth and belief in Christ—*that He would do for you what you observe—creates what you receive.*

We tap into Jesus' perfect set of energetic frequencies and put our faith in action to be in sync with His divine energy. We could say the distorted waves of sickness change when our waves ride on the waves of Jesus, reforming the body systems into divine waves of energy. There is no imperfect energy and no distorted energy within Jesus. He can't put sickness in you. Satan carries and administers the distorted frequencies of sin's energy. God, Jesus, and the Holy Spirit have no sin and nothing imperfect within them. This is why Satan had to talk to God about Job.

In my humble opinion, I don't think Satan had as much legal right to inflict Job to the degree that he did. We give the enemy legal agreement to inflict our lives by comingling with his energies, his nature. He can even get legal right of entry to us from previous generational sins. That is what makes me think Satan had to get permission from God to inflict as much as God would allow upon Job. We know that God allowed anything but killing him. I don't presume to know what was totally in the mind of God to allow what he did in Job's life. This is just my thought and I am thankful for the extreme example of Job when I think I am going through bad circumstances.

Only God knows what we can handle and Job is not the normal for everyone to go through.

You could say you work your thoughts of energy by telling yourself to make a heart connection, which conforms to what you believe Jesus already possesses for you. He has all of your healing and miracles of energy because He created everything and holds all things together. In the case of the woman, scripture says she talked to herself. Matthew 9:21 says, "For *she said within herself*, If I may but touch his garment, I shall be whole. "

I desire to paint pictures in your mind that will make a heart connection with supernaturally wide brush strokes that will forever change the negative pictures and beliefs in your memories. Now is a perfect time to stretch your mind to pop a qwiff. (Read Isaiah 54.)

Now stop and think for a moment. How far away from you do you think your miracle, healing, or change is? Change is something you cause, not the cosmos doing it for you. God wants to see His image come out of you. You take heaven and bring it to earth. You can change how you observe your health, or how you observe your life in Jesus. What are you choosing to believe to observe in your thoughts? Realize that it is available to you in a nanosecond, which is one billionth of a second. To say Jesus is close is an understatement.

Your Present is Your Future Now

Are you really getting what you are capable of? What you perceive to be, you receive because you get what you observe. Popping a qwiff is the function of what you are observing in thoughts to cause them to be. This is called *quantum electrodynamics*. It's also known as taking a quantum leap—leaping by causing something to be, as you observed it to be in your thinking. You cause the future by how you observe the future, in the nanoseconds coming into your life in your present. Your present is your future now.

Are you "seeing" what I am saying? Do you see what I said earlier about possibilities being in your present and that the future is your present? This is taking place in your thought life, by what you perceive, what you observe something to be. Who are you listening to in your physical environment and from the invisible environment, that is affecting you? Who do you want to listen to? You make the choice. Do you know God's plan for your tomorrow? You can find out when you seek Him.

Quantum physics has discovered a subatomic particle of light that moves faster than the speed of light as we know it. Science refers to it as a tachyon. They don't like tachyons because they can't be explained, but that doesn't change the fact that they exist.

Gerald Feinberg, a young scientist who studied the blackboards of Einstein's formulas, found this subatomic particle that moves faster than the speed of light in all matter. Remember, our bodies are made up of matter which is light energy. They also found that when this particle gave up its energy, it appeared at all points across its trajectory, or its flight path. God is present everywhere at the same time—omnipresent. I believe they found the Holy Spirit.

God is outside of this time and space. In time and space as we know it, light only travels up to the speed of light, (186,000 miles per hour) but light travels faster than that in eternity. God travels faster than the speed of light in the spirit realm. When we receive revelation prophecy which speaks of the future, it is information that comes to us faster than the speed of light.

If science has found something moving faster than the speed of light and they found that it appears at all points across a trajectory path, then that also means you can know God has been at all points in your life before you. He knows the beginning from the end. Revelation 1:8 says, "I am Alpha and Omega, the beginning and the ending, saith the Lord, which is, and which was, and which is to come, the Almighty." God is moving in everything, everywhere at the same time. He has experienced every circumstance you are going through or ever will go through, and stands ready to declare to you the things that are to come for you.

John 16:13 says, "But when He, the Spirit of Truth (the Truth-giving Spirit) comes, He will guide you into all the Truth (the whole, full Truth). For He will not speak His own message [on His own authority]; but He will tell whatever He hears [from the Father; He will give the message that has been given to Him], and He will announce and declare to you the things that are to come [that will happen in the future]" (AMP).

With God's power and authority, we have been given the power to tap into the spirit to create our future. This is why it is impossible to please God without faith. Just as Hebrews 11:6 says, "But without faith it is impossible to please him: for he that cometh to God must believe that he is and that he is a rewarder of them that diligently seek him." He has designed life to happen with our active involvement because He created us to speak what is in our hearts to create it. We have the ability to use our thoughts to observe and perceive what we see and to make it our physical reality.

We fill ourselves with life when we perceive with positive emotions because positive emotional natures have energies that contain light for creating something new and good. If we use negative emotions, those energies tear down and distort the positive energy that is present bringing death into our lives.

God has given us all the promises and paid off all of our debts on the cross. He didn't give us disease, or put sickness on us. Satan does this by taking the waves of energy we have that are good and distorting them for bad. Psalm 103:3 says He heals us of "all" our diseases: "Who forgiveth all thine iniquities; who healeth all thy diseases." Isaiah 53:5 also says, "But he was wounded for our transgressions, he was bruised for our iniquities: the chastisement of our peace was upon him; and with his stripes we are healed." Finally, First Peter 2:24 says, "Who his own self bare our sins in his own body on the tree that we, being dead to sins, should live unto righteousness: by whose stripes ye were healed." These few scriptures tell us that we "are" healed of "all" diseases, not some but all. That is both mental and physical diseases. The condition is to ask Him to forgive us of our iniquities.

Now with this always comes the question of why everyone doesn't receive healing. God usually gets blamed when that happens. For the sake of sparing you the debate that comes from many schools of thought. The way I look at this question is to ask the question, "Who knows the thoughts of the heart and mind of a person, except the person themselves and God?" No one knows the thoughts of men but God. The person doesn't even know all his or her own thoughts, but God knows every thought we house. Our non-conscious mind has thoughts even we aren't aware of unless they are revealed to us by God for redemption and deliverance. We aren't conscious of every thought. All I know is that I don't want to call God a liar when His word clearly says that He sent His Son to heal us by His stripes. He took upon Himself "all" our diseases.

Most of what happens or doesn't happen for us has to do with a lack of knowledge, both regarding our enemy in this world and regarding who we really are in the full position of authority in the Lord. First, this causes us to be ignorant of how to battle and overcome him, which we alone must do because no one else can do it for us. Second, it causes us to be ignorant of whom we really are in our position and authority in the Kingdom of God.

There are two major reasons why the enemy, the prince of the power of the air, continues to deceive us. Sadly, we are ill-equipped for the war. Second Corinthians 10:4 says our weapons aren't seen physically: "For the weapons of our warfare are not physical [weapons of flesh and blood], but they are mighty before God for the overthrow and destruction of strongholds" (AMP). Yet how many realize what is happening to them that is invisible to their eyes?

In fact, once you look at your world from an invisible energetic view, you see it is impossible for God to use vibrational distorted frequencies which cause disease and sickness. God has no imperfection and no sin frequencies of energy within His being. Mental and physical diseases are distorted frequencies of energy that cause a breakdown in your organs and your nervous system. This is impossible for God to do "to" you. We need to see who really does this through us and stop blaming God for the bad things that happen to us. He is a good God who wants to give good gifts to us. He provides His word to train us and give us an understanding of how we should choose to live life whole.

Satan is full of darkness of evil. He comes to steal our light to bring us into the darkness with him. Satan, who was created by God to be the bearer of light, had chosen to fill himself with iniquity, with darkness of evil. He has no light within him anywhere anymore. Second Corinthians 11:14 says that Satan can come *"as"* an angel of light to us: "And it is no wonder, for Satan himself *"masquerades as"* an angel of light." He is no longer the bearer of light. Jesus refers to him as darkness that can effect our lives in John 12:35,

"Then Jesus said unto them, Yet a little while is the light with you. Walk while ye have the light, lest darkness come upon you: for he that walketh in darkness knoweth not whither he goeth." And in Second Corinthians 6:14, "Be ye not unequally yoked together with unbelievers: for what fellowship hath righteousness with unrighteousness? And what communion hath light with darkness?"

Evil is made up of low distorted vibrational frequencies of energy. God has all the energies of light with life in them and Satan, along with one third of the angels who chose to follow him, have only distorted vibrational frequencies of energy. When evil energy intersects with God's kingdom of lighted energy, it distorts it. This ability is given to Satan's kingdom when we give him permission to mess with us.

The minute we agree with what evil says to us, we are calling God a liar and it puts us in harmony (in unity), with evil and separates us from God. Sin happens when we take it to the final step of acting the evil energy out. That happens when we observe it, which begins in our thinking. When we focus on it in thought, to observe it happening, we are in the beginning stages of creating a reality. You are incubating.

This is why Jesus said that when you lust upon a woman to commit adultery, you have already sinned in your heart against God. Matthew 5:28, "But I say unto you, That whosoever looketh on a woman to lust after her hath committed adultery with her already in his heart."

This is why our enemy wants to program and play with our perceptions. He works to coerce and deceive us into thinking and believing as he does. This action will grow us into taking on his natures, by our agreement with what he is speaking to us in our thoughts. This causes us to disbelieve what God says, which separates us from Him in the spirit. Satan distorts the light energies in us so he can diminish the amount of light in the earth, which changes things in the earth to the way he wants them.

This is done through man because man is the devil's only access point into this earth for manifesting what he desires. We carry the light of God in this earth. But God accesses the earth through us also. Philippians 2:15 says, "That ye may be blameless and harmless, the sons of God, without rebuke, in the midst of a crooked and perverse nation, among whom ye shine as lights in the world."

God used Satan to point out Job. God does not have the ability to put any evil, sinful natures like fear, pride, hate, jealousy, unforgiveness, bitterness, and others into us because God is without sin. God used Satan to expose to Job what was on the inside of Job. God wanted to reveal to Job what He had packaged into him when He created him, by exposing what was inside him that had crept in since then. I am not God, nor do I presume to know why He chose to do that with Job, but that isn't my point here. I raise this purely to illustrate that God cannot give sin energies to you. Sin is not found within God. But He can and does use the devices of Satan.

God wants us to discover Himself in us and He wants to discover and unpack Himself to us, for Himself. There is a bigger picture here that He has created and that is playing out on earth. We have the greater power in us. Greater is He (God) that is in us than he (Satan) who is in this world. First John 4:4 says, "Ye are of God, little children, and have overcome them: because greater is he that is in you, than he that is in the world."

Those frequencies of darkness and distortion are what Satan has messed with for thousands of years to cause dysfunction and death. Satan has set out to tear down all that God creates. He is the one to blame for what is wrong in your life. He is distorting man's light to create evil without them even knowing because they lack knowledge.

We spend more time speaking to things that "are," as though they "are not" (causing them to not be), canceling out all possibilities. We were designed to call the things that are "not" as though they "are." That is why God "desires" to "need" us. He packed all possibilities, abilities, powers, and creativity into us, with only one condition. All other conditions are based off of this one ultimately important condition first. It is found in Mark 12:30: "And thou shalt *love* the Lord thy God with all thy heart, and with all thy soul, and with all thy mind, and with all thy strength: this is the first commandment. And the second is like, namely this, Thou shalt *love* thy neighbor as thyself. There is none other commandment greater than these."

Faith must be worked from love within us if we want what we create to be positive and good. Galatians 5:6 says, "For in Jesus Christ neither circumcision availeth any thing, nor uncircumcision; but faith which worketh by love." Faith without works is dead. James 2:17, "Even so faith, if it hath not works, is dead, being alone."

Nothing is impossible to you if you work your faith in God. Matthew 17:20 says, "And Jesus said unto them, Because of your unbelief: for verily I say unto you, If ye have faith as a grain of mustard seed, ye shall say unto this mountain, Remove hence to yonder place; and it shall remove; and nothing shall be impossible unto you. Remember Hebrews 11:1: "Now faith is the substance of things hoped for, the evidence of things not seen."

Faith demands to be fulfilled, either way, for good or for bad. Faith is the substance of things hoped for and the evidence of things not seen "until" we do the work by observing before it becomes something we experience and see it in the physical world. It is the invisible motion of energies from which things get created. Future possibilities flow from the invisible motion to you.

Chapter 15

Perception Deceptions

Perception involves seeing beyond the visible, to see with both the physical senses and what is in the spirit. It does require faith to believe for what will be created in the next moments that are coming to us either way; good or bad. Perception involves thoughts that have created beliefs and if our beliefs are wrong, we will have misperceptions. Always remember, misperceptions can be reprogrammed.

Thoughts and beliefs are invisible motion within us. We can't see them with our five senses until we paint them. It's like when an artist sees a garden full of flowers. Only when he paints the garden on a canvas is the garden brought into existence. Likewise, what you perceive within yourself you must put onto a canvas so you can see it with your physical senses. This can be done by painting, writing, drawing, or by words. The most used brush for painting on canvas is the brush of WORDS. We paint our perceptions on a canvas faster with words than any other method. So many people do not even know what their words are doing. This is why we have to speak what we want to see by faith. Speak out to canceling any negative words you have spoken, to void them.

Man was made in God's image. "Image" means "to reveal." God splashed His image across the entire universe. He took what He observed and painted, sculpted, and used His word to bring it into existence. Perception requires seeing something inside you that wants to be brought into existence outside of you. This is how you get others to view your perception, to see things the way you see them, so they can experience what you are experiencing. Kim Clement says, "You've got to say what you hear so you can see what you've said." Paint your words onto a canvas so you can see what you heard. (See Kim Clement's series called *Perception*.) Some of these thoughts on perception are from his series.

God made man to *reveal* what he *observes* or perceives. He really created man to reveal Himself—God in the earth. We all gain knowledge from the environment by the act of perceiving and then bringing it into existence so others can see the perception we do.

None of us would have much knowledge of the environment we are living in if it weren't for our sharing of perceptions with one another. This is how we are able to experience what others experience. God intends this to be for the helping, caring, and loving of one another. This is a way we love our neighbor as ourselves.

This means that whatever new perception you are opposed to seeing, because of a previously stored perception that does not agree with it, you disqualified yourself from putting it onto a canvas for others to perceive. You won't create what you saw. This new perception can be true and the old stored one can be false.

The only accurate way to reprogram false perceptions is to see if they say what God says. True perceptions are going to possess qualities and natures that are expressions of God which come forth when we choose to activate our positive control systems with positive emotions. These perceptions will resonate from your heart and cause harmony with your mind, thus renewing your mind.

Do you see how our beliefs get created by our perceptions? Do you realize that we all have many false perceptions that need to be renewed or reprogrammed? This is why the changing of a false belief, or removal of a bad memory, requires a synchronization with perfect energy waves. That happens when we harmonize with positive emotional energy waves. As we illustrated earlier, our binding together with those waves (like a braided rope), or riding the waves of those positive energies is what transforms the distorted, dysfunctional waves of negative energies.

This is why it doesn't do any good to dwell on our past negative hurts or the circumstances of our current negative environment. Nothing will change for us when we do this. The waves of distortion remain to distort positive energy. It will not work to dwell on our past or present sins either, therefore, repent and immediately go back to activating your positive control system or positive emotional natures. When you have a sin consciousness all the time, you see "self" instead of seeing God in you. Your focus is on self. What you are consciously aware of the most is what you will see both inside and outside of you.

This is also why discussing with someone all of the bad that has happened in your life will only keep that reinforced in your programming. Why? Think of it this way: whatever you think on, those energies of emotions will cause you to become them. As a man thinks, so he becomes. You are actively harmonizing with those distorted, dysfunctional frequency patterns. Those energies will never change until you actively bring into your thoughts energy waves that are emotionally positive in nature. The energies you keep harmonizing with will multiply and manifest their nature in you. Whatever energy you vibrate like, is how you vibrate also.

Words Send out Images

Words are more powerful than we seem to want to understand. Your words send out images that create the whole perception. Spoken words throw images out onto the airspace canvas—they have invisible motion. Anyone in the physical can take those words of images in but so can any spirit being take those words and use them to paint on mental canvases in mankind. Words are thoughts; thoughts are images.

These images consist of light energy or dark energy. For example, if you saw someone paint on their canvas that it was normal for women to be taken advantage of, guess what you will paint to bring into existence on your canvas, unless you choose to believe the opposite perception? If you saw a canvas that showed the perception of verbal abuse being okay to speak, what do you think you will bring into existence with the brush of words on your canvas unless you believe and paint with your words the opposite, positive perception?

You take control and change your perceptions from positive to negative in order to change what you originally chose to believe. You presuppose what you want to see on the outside of you by taking what you see on the inside of you and speaking it outside of you.

Some might say that sounds like pretending because you do not physically see what you are saying. Pretending is thinking and never saying or doing a thing about what you're thinking. Presupposing involves activating your faith to call things that are not as though they were. This is why you will not see a thing at first. Just like the farmer who plants his seed in the ground, then has to wait whatever time it takes for the plant to be seen. If he plants a field of corn, does he stop thinking after the first day or first week that corn isn't going to appear? Of course not! He even makes sure that the field gets watered, knowing full well that corn will appear. He would never dream of spreading poison on the field before he waited for the plant to appear.

We however, often throw our seed out (by our words) and just because we don't see what we planted by our words in the time we expect, we throw poisonous words on top of the seed and kill our harvest.

Our enemy knows how to work his presuppositions into us every day. He takes stored beliefs from perceptions and presupposes something he wants to have you do or not do. He has been busy working on this since before you were even born. For example, say he programmed into you as a child the fact that you can't do anything right. He then presupposes that you won't become the leader of a nation, or the CEO of a profitable business. How does he do that? He speaks with his words and puts images into you from those stored images you experienced from not doing anything right. He then gives you the faith to believe from those stored images that you can't become someone who can do things right, or be successful. He presupposes your future off a false perception programmed into you as a child.

If we allow it, Satan will get us to operate in his darkness by faith all day long. Then when we want to speak out onto a different canvas that which we see inside of us that says we are a mighty man or woman of God who will be used by Him to change people's hearts and minds, thus setting them free, what thoughts do you think will come along, perhaps even before we speak those words?

The enemy comes and speaks to us, telling us we are crazy or not realistic and question whether God can even use us. Pretend all you want, but it's not happening. After all, is that what you see in the physical? Satan calls you stupid for saying something that makes no sense with what you see now. You are in debt up to your eyeballs and you are speaking that you are debt free and lack for nothing? Or you are speaking out that you are healed because you see and believe that on the inside of you, though on the outside you still have that disease and it doesn't seem to be getting better.

Speaking in faith is presupposing that what you see and believe on the inside needs an external canvas to be painted upon so the working of your faith energies will become physical. They are always internal before they become external. Doesn't the Word tell us to call things that are NOT as though they ARE? Satan has us calling things that ARE as though they are NOT, and we don't even get intimidated into speaking that negative stuff with our word brush.

The opposite will start to take place via the voice of God that comes out of you, the voice that dictates what is inside your spirit, that you are to speak to the earthly manifestations, causing those energies to align with what is in your spirit from God. It is calling things as though they are. What is in your spirit is opposite from what your body is experiencing in the natural. If you can speak out of your spirit the opposite of what you are experiencing in the natural, you will transform your circumstances by faith. This action causes things to become, which is why it is impossible to please God without faith. We are designed to work our faith in His love.

God's access into the earth realm is through us. Adam kicked access to God off the planet. Jesus, the word of God, brought the access to God back to earth. Whatever happens here on earth has got to come through us, *by our words*. We carry His voice, and you better believe Satan is threatened by us because of it.

The enemy speaks words into our heads methodically to try and undo our positive control system. His words send out images that create the whole negative perception in you. He does it without us even having full knowledge of what is happening and we are held captive *by those images*. He starts his programming before we are even born. He takes further advantage of us up to the age of six, trying to hard-wire false perceptions into our memories. We pass on perceptions that were passed on to us, not knowing any better, and so the cycle repeats down through the family line.

My people perish for lack of knowledge, God says. Here is why: "For God, who commanded the light to shine out of darkness, hath shined in our hearts, to give the light of the knowledge of the glory of God in the face of Jesus Christ" (2 Corinthians 4:6). Here is why the enemy steals light from us. The more knowledge we receive from God, the greater weight of glory we receive. The light is in the knowledge and the knowledge reveals the glory of God in us. God has already put it there—we are made in His image and likeness. There is knowledge in us that hasn't received light yet.

Second Corinthians 4:7 says, "we have this treasure in earthen vessels (our bodies are earthen vessels), that the excellency of the power may be of God, and not of us." The treasure is the glory of God. God gave you a treasure, intending for it to come out. A part of Him is inside of you.

Second Corinthians 4:8-9 goes on to say, "We are troubled on every side, yet not distressed; we are perplexed, but not in despair; Persecuted, but not forsaken; cast down, but not destroyed." If you are hard pressed but not crushed these things it is not a problem. These things are causing you to engage your positive control system to increase with energy carrying light which brings a greater weight of God's glory out of you. These things give you a greater weight of glory to shine out of you, resulting in a greater voice that will paint a bigger canvas—just waiting to come out of you to reflect God and affect others around you.

Second Corinthians 4:10 speaks of the fact that the life of Jesus is manifested in our body in the world around us. These things are causing a manifestation of Jesus through us. However, in Second Corinthians 4:17, we are assured affliction is but for a moment and working for us a greater weight of glory. This works "for" you, so you have a stronger and stronger gifting within you.

We learned earlier how the heart has an energy field that exudes outside of the body. Have you ever noticed someone who walks into a room and the atmosphere changes for the positive? It is because there is more of the light of glory resonating from that person. Just as grapes are pressed to get the juice out of them, so we receive more weight of glory when we gain knowledge and go through hardship. It teaches us to draw from the inward connections we make with the positive emotional energies of the positive control system from God.

Even though our outward man might be affected by this, our inward man, or spirit man is being renewed day by day. Second Corinthians 4:16 tells us this, "For which cause we faint not; but though our outward man perish, yet the inward man is renewed day by day." If you can speak out of your spirit the opposite of what you are experiencing in the natural, you will change your circumstances.

God is looking for our perceptions to match the images that He put within us when He created us in His mind. Kim teaches that when two images match, meaning when we see ourselves as God sees us, we then have an optical fusion. When two images join they become one perception and the two become one. It is the correct blending of the images of both the eye of God with our spiritual eye. You can do anything you have the ability to see (observe). God wants this to be an optical fusion between you and Him and wants you to see yourself how He sees you. We don't even know what we look like until He shows us who He created us to be.

It became more "natural" to see the visible facts with our five senses. You might say that Satan caused an "incorrect" optical fusion by painting with words what he perceived, causing man to see what he saw. Words are what he used and still uses, to paint word pictures, to cause a deposit of his image into the mind of man. And once man accepted that perception as his new truth, the two images fused together as one. He has observed and studied for thousands of years how God created man in His own image and likeness. He understands how to twist the very things God intended for good, so they are used for evil and sin.

God's Math is Quantum

We operate off of stored beliefs we acquired through circumstances. This may seem scary, when you think about how, or even if, you will break free from or change all the falsehood stored in you. Good news! Know that the stronger power of energy comes from the positive operating system within you.

God's "math" is off the charts when it comes to making changes. The Word says that one can put a thousand to flight, and 2 can put 10,000 to flight. Run that math a little further and you will see that 3 can put 100,000 to flight; 4 can put 1,000,000 (one million) to flight; 5 can put 10,000,000 (ten million) to flight; 6 can put 100,000,000 (one hundred million) to flight; 7 can put 1,000,000,000 (one billion) to flight, and; 10 puts a trillion to flight. This is God's quantum math. Remember quantum means radiant energies. The devil's kingdom is no match for the Kingdom of God. The key is knowing that the Kingdom of God is in you and how to operate in it.

So what does God mean by "putting to flight"? That means putting to flight Satan's kingdom of fallen angels, powers, and principalities. Who are they, or shall I say, what are they? They are beings full of negative powers of distorted energies with dysfunctional natures of evil. So that means what Satan has spent a lifetime downloading into you, through Jesus (the Word of God), can be rapidly removed or reprogrammed. How? By activating the positive operating system within you, which is to say, activating the positive emotional energies that originate from what the Word speaks. The more consistent and diligent you are about using His Words, the sooner you will become an overcomer. Remember that through neuroplasticity the brain has the natural ability to form new connections in order to compensate for injury or changes in one's environment God has wonderfully equipped us for all things to be possible with Him in us.

How God's Spoken Word Transforms

This is what the word of God speaks about in Ephesians 5 as the washing by the word. It washes the old images and changes them into the images of God. It is changing your internal energy to resonate in harmony with God's stronger waves of energies. This transforms the distorted energy of memories within you into positive emotional natures that the Word teaches us are ours to possess to overcome anything negative.

When we *observe* what the Word says, the Word *speaks to our heart*. Remember *the way a perception is shared is by painting it, drawing it, writing it, or speaking it so it can be seen and experienced by someone else*. We share an interpretation of an event to hard-wire beliefs, thoughts and feelings which lead to emotions.

The written Word speaks of perceptions that are truth and it paints images on a canvas both for us to see that truth and to experience what truth is. The images it holds are deposited in our thoughts to change an old false stored image. When our image matches the image sent through the Word, we have an optical fusion—two becoming one. The old one is gone, totally erased. The enemy tricks us by bringing up our past. He does this to keep those images of past failures hard-wired as negative false beliefs of who we were. Every time he does that, we need to dismiss him by reminding him of his future!

Review

Remember we must allow the connection to die and not rewire itself by refocusing on the old false belief. It will be natural for it to want to get rewired. Remember to keep kicking the old thought of belief out. Remember to make a new habit of doing this with consistency for twenty one days.

We now understand that everything is made up of energy at its core. Thoughts are made up of energy and so on. All new images created by positive energies of light cancel out the distorted negative energies of darkness—the old has become new. Where light enters, it dispels the darkness. The transforming of our thinking, in our mind, has been renewed from a false perception and belief into a true belief and perception.

The more we do this washing of the energy from the Word, the more rapidly we cancel old images and create new ones in their place. We become more like God because we carry and resonate more of His nature. The more we carry of His nature, the more we will reflect or express His nature, we resonate it outward into our surrounding environment.

This is dangerous for the enemy because this means that we end up canceling out more and more of his distorted negative energy

–that which hold his perceptions for evil. This causes dysfunction for him and he no longer has a hold on us. This is what Jesus did for us to have life when He got the keys back from Satan, ending the hold of death and reign of Satan over earth he enjoyed prior to Jesus' death.

Satan severed the connection man had in the spirit in the garden. Before that, man's spirit was one with God's spirit. After Jesus died and His blood was spilled on this earth to pay for our sin against God, we gained access through His Holy Spirit to become one in spirit again with Him. Satan bluffs us into thinking that he holds the energetic power to rule and reign on earth, but he can't do a thing without using us to do it...and his days are numbered.

The Enemy Sees you the Way you See Yourself

Satan comes to change the view of ourselves to match his perception. *The greater you see yourself in Christ, the greater Satan sees you and the more afraid he is to confront you. Others see us the way we see ourselves. He tries to diminish you in your thoughts, to change your beliefs of who you are by attacking you through your past weaknesses, mistakes, and sins.*

How do others and Satan's kingdom see us as we see ourselves? You are a transmitter. Look at it this way. The more we see ourselves in Christ, (the way Christ sees us) the more we transmit His combination of frequencies. When Satan looks at us, he sees how much light you put off and by what he feels. God's love energies and other frequencies of His nature like kindness, caring, appreciation, goodness, forgiveness, giving, etc., when transmitted by us cause him to feel tormented. His evil vibrations need to be calmed down by pulling the light out and off of us. With the light turning to darkness within us, the enemy feels less tormented because the frequencies of vibration aren't in opposition to his vibrations.

The more we see ourselves like Christ sees us, the greater we become an invisible neon sign increasing with His light in us. That is why the more light of God's glory (His weight of glory) you carry in you, the more torment you cause to the kingdom of darkness. You must also understand that just like Jesus when He was on earth, with that greater weight of glory light, more enemy chaos will come into your life. We were created to overcome chaos, to resolve problems.

We like the word God gives us to take dominion but do we forget that He said for us to subdue every living thing that moves on the earth. Genesis 1:28, "And God blessed them, and God said unto them, Be fruitful, and multiply, and replenish the earth, and *subdue it: and have dominion* over the fish of the sea, and over the fowl of the air, and *over every living thing that moveth upon the earth.*" God knew that Satan would influence mankind to act like himself and that mankind would have to be equipped to subdue him. God created man and woman for conflict resolution, with the ability to subdue and to take dominion on the earth. We need to tap into His kingdom to do it. Mankind runs from conflict and demonic chaos largely because they don't know what or where their weapons are located. They are available inside you, in Christ.

It is vital to see yourself as God intends for you to see yourself. Otherwise you will walk around being defeated when you are called and equipped to be an overcomer. This is how the enemy sees you the way you see yourself.

Satan uses words to paint a canvas of his perception which he wants you to observe, perceive and accept as truth about yourself— that you are not worthy, or can't accomplish something good that you want because of something you did in your past. Perhaps he tells you that you won't make it. He knows you are agreeing with him when you speak that negative perception of yourself. He tries to get you to do this over and over again until a false perception about yourself becomes what you believe to be the truth.

We all take a perception we believe is truth, even if it is false, and tell it to ourselves and others by hitting the repeat button of our memory recording system. Until we perceive something, we have no experience of it or awareness of it. Satan needs to weaken you so he can gain a foothold in you. Why? Because he knows that what you perceive you will receive and he certainly doesn't want you to become strong in the word so you know the truth God says about you.

Get a Grip on What is Happening

Stop right here. Do you see what is happening? I will paint on a canvas what Satan is up to. The perceptions we paint for ourselves to see again, or to share with others, are stored interpretations of events we have both experienced and learned to believe. They are images of us that we look at. Even if they are as false as false can get, we still look at them and learn to believe in what we see. Now take a look at what Satan is really doing when he paints with words in your thoughts.

He is speaking about himself. He is painting on the canvas of your mind for you to observe who "he" believes himself to be. *He wants you to be made over by him, into his image.* God created you in His image and Satan wants to replace the image of God in you with his image. He knows that if you have more of his image, you will carry his nature to reflect him onto others. You will worship him and idolize all he is. He aims for the very core of your being relentlessly in everything he does.

You end up observing a false perception, a false image of you, because it is a picture of him. He painted his perception, his belief that he holds of himself, for you to observe. Maybe you did copy that image of him into yourself by acting like him in the past, but the awareness you need is that you can decide to change your perceptions and all those negative false beliefs of yourself by getting a grip on what is happening in you.

Research has shown that the same hormones that trigger joy also trigger anger (epinephrine, norepinephrine, and thyrotropic hormone). What makes the same hormones unleash these two opposite emotions is our perceptions and our interpretation of what caused the event. We become angered when we perceive a threat and full of joy when we perceive love. We feel connectedness or oneness with something or someone that brings us joy.

So what is the significance of this? Just that Satan hasn't created any new physiological dysfunctions within our system. He simply uses what God put there when He created man and subjects our systems to enough perceived threats and fears for a long enough period of time to distort the growth frequencies of energies that reside within Christ. He causes disharmony with Jesus in our system via our thoughts, causing us to perceive what we receive.

Satan creates nothing new. I repeat; Satan creates nothing new in the universe. He simply transmits the distorted frequencies of energy; all he was left with from his rebellion and disobedience toward God. He uses these even now to try and cause the love energies of God to become dysfunctional. All we need to realize is that we, as God's children, can choose to harmonize with Jesus, the word of God, and bring our operating systems back into alignment and congruency, in sync with our built-in positive emotional operating system.

We can create new images and new perceptions which in turn, hard-wire new beliefs into us. When we choose to do this "first" (because God doesn't force anyone to do anything), the events that come into our lives reinforce those new beliefs. The more we operate in those new perceptions, the more events we will experience that match those new beliefs. Why? Because whatever energy we act with, we create the events and experiences that harmonize with those energies. "Like attracts like" is a universal law. You don't exist without harmonizing with something every moment you are living. Everything created is resonating, harmonizing, and singing with either good or bad. If anything created on earth stops vibrating with energy, it is dead.

King David is about the best example of how someone engaged his positive control system to sing his song in harmony with the Lord. David sought diligently to have his heart beat in sync and in tune with God's. He also taught others to do the same. Back then, they didn't know what we do today in terms of the science and the biology of what that harmony does for our well-being. In light of this knowledge, it doesn't surprise me that God said David was a man after His own heart. He experienced what it was to get high in the spirit of oneness with God. He had a heart seeking to stay congruent with God's heart.

David looked for God's vibrations in sound to become in unity to sing. This is why I believe King David talked so much about singing and sang to the Lord—even to the point of dancing naked.

His entire body got involved with being congruent with the heart of God. He lost himself in the harmonies of the love of the Lord.

The higher the level of synchronicity with God, the more we become addicted to His love vibrations. That addiction is the only addiction that won't harm us but which will fulfill us at the very core of our body, soul, and spirit. It is also why I believe he would not harm Saul, even when Saul kept trying to kill him, again and again. It is also the very reason why Paul was tortured by evil ever-present around him, yet he kept writing encouragement to the church of Corinth. It is why any of the great men and women of faith in the Bible endured what they did. The harmony they experienced with God sustained them and made it worth what they had to endure.

If <u>*you perceive yourself*</u> as mighty in Christ to the pulling down of strongholds he has laid within you, that gives you dominion over Satan and any weapon he wants to use against you. Dominion is the issue. Knowing, and becoming aware of your authority in Christ, is the understanding all of us need to overcome life challenges.

Jesus, after He died on earth, went to hell with the superpower energies of love and got legal access to the earth realm once again, through man, to rule and reign. We now have the ability to engage and become one with this energetic power of God, through the Holy Spirit in us. We can use it to destroy the enemy in and around us. We need the Holy Spirit to reveal God's word to us every day, so we might know what is going on in the invisible realm of the spirit. If we don't have communion with Him every day, we are just as the blind man who lives in darkness, sitting in the middle of a war zone. Have you ever felt like that? I know I have.

Love Is the Superpower of All

Love is the ultimate superpower of all energy. What makes me say that? God *"IS"* love. There is nothing that can stand up to love's energetic power. It is the most powerful, energetic force in God and in the universe He created. He wants us to engage and become one with that power, so as to transform all the distorted, dysfunctional energy of our enemy. That is why He made love the most important commandment, telling us to love the Lord your God with all your heart, soul, and strength, and to love your neighbor as yourself. We are unaware of the hidden potential that lies within us because He is inside of us waiting to become one.

Everything has God's energy and that includes you. God is available to you in every situation you face. To deny that is to deny that God exists in everything, everywhere at all times. His invisible energy is constantly in you and surrounding you. Why? The kingdom of God is in you. His energy also makes up "all" things. All the enemy is doing is distorting the energy of God. He uses and abuses what is God's. At any moment, no matter what is going on in your life, you have the ability to activate, or hook up to the positive control system in you.

God's emotional energies of love, kindness, caring, appreciation, gratitude, and all the rest are far greater and more powerful than the enemy's energetic ability to distort God's energy. God wants to unpack His power that is inside of you, the power that He placed in you when you were originally created in His mind.

We think we are lost but He never leaves us and will not allow us to stumble. The Holy Spirit stays in the throne room of our heart. Once we accept Him into our heart as our Savior, He never moves from that position. There is only one way to move Him out—become full of iniquity, just like Lucifer.

We can't always hear God speak when the enemy is clamoring too loudly with the chaos around us but one thing is for sure, He is always, always there. He is waiting for a state of purposed peace, so He can speak and we can hear. Why the state of peace? Because we purpose ourselves to come to Him and when we do, we resonate, harmonize, and become in sync with His sounds. Then we can hear more clearly. Whatsoever is _____, think on these things. Fill in the blank with all positive emotions, because they are all of God.

All negative emotions are distorted energetic vibrations that Satan's kingdom transmits. These can cause the positive emotional energies of God to become dysfunctional in our thinking and in our physiology.

Our thoughts harmonize with either the negative control system (negative emotions) or the positive control system (positive emotions) in us. We build our positive control system stronger by the amount of time we spend meditating on His Word of Truth. This grows our spirit with more light. More light to overpower the darkness. Unfortunately the opposite is also true. If we spend more time with negative meditative thinking, the negative control system is more active in us. That means the darkness is greater and strengthened in its ability to snuff the light out of you.

Survival mode or Growth mode

We must spend time where we receive light. You can know if you are spending, or being affected by too much darkness with this test. If you feel like your life is mostly made up of the need to protect yourself, you are doing that because you are fighting darkness. Why? The darker it gets in our lives, the more our automatic will to survive is activated, protecting and defending us from all perceived threats, both mental and physical. Why? We were created to either be in survival mode or growth mode, and it is impossible to be in both modes at the same time. That is like trying to be in forward and reverse at the same time, it is impossible.

What that means is when you are surviving, you are not growing. Your cells just try to balance the imbalance that is caused when you are in survival mode. They cannot grow and produce with proper balance what every organ and system of your body requires. This means that the more time you spend on surviving life, the greater your bodily functions are over working to try to find balance. This has its consequences over time.

Therefore, the only solution is to overcome the darkness by grabbing hold of the light. We do this by activating our positive control system which holds more power than the negative control system. We do this by spending time meditating on positive emotions and finding ways to act with them. As we do this, we resonate, harmonize, and are in tune with positive energies and the distorted energies change. It isn't good enough to just think about positive emotions. We need to engage our whole physiology in that process. It also has to involve what we are giving off.

The most powerful source for such thoughts is the word of God because it is full of life and breath of light. Why is that? It's not Joe's words, Jane's words, or Bill's words—it is the word of God, from which everything that exists came into being. It is the voice of God that spoke through men who perceived Him and painted a canvas for us to observe. After they saw the picture, they became one with God's beliefs.

Light dispels the darkness. The darker an area is, the more light it will require to dispel the darkness. It will require more hours of the positive control system to be turned on. (We turn these systems on or off.) We can influence each other by what we paint on our word canvas, where others can perceive what we perceive and believe.

Some may say, "But you don't know what I live with and have to put up with! How can it be all up to me? How can it possibly be up to me to change someone else, or to make them stop saying hurtful things?" You are right; you cannot make someone else stop what they are saying to you.

It is up to each of us individually to decide what we are going to agree to listen to and put up with. Sometimes that involves making a choice of what environment we stay in. The choices of what has happened to us always lie with us, not the other person. We choose to either perceive what someone else does or says to us as truth, or we can walk away from it and decide not to agree with it or to put up with it.

Humans Emit a Unique Energy with Intent

Non-conscious operating processes, or stored memories, can be altered when we become *consciously aware* of our intent. We do this by making a conscious choice of what we want to change. Then the patterns of energy are altered in our immune system (for the healing of sickness, for example). Once again, one putting a thousand to flight and two putting ten thousand to flight comes into operation.

In *Healing with Love,* by Leonard Laskow, he tells of William Tiller, a professor at Stanford University. In 1986, Tiller reported that he developed and tested a device that released electrons when healing was the subject of intent when it was used. He tested the device by telling individuals to intentionally focus healing energy into the device through their hands. As long as they kept their focused intent toward the device for healing, the device registered electron counts after ninety seconds for a five minute period. (Electrons are negatively charged particles of energy.) More than fifty thousand bursts were recorded. When the intent was discontinued, gradually the registered energy bursts subsided.

Tiller then neutralized his intent by focusing on math calculations. No energy bursts were registered by the device at all. He also discovered that if he was ill or not clear minded the electron counts were much lower than when he was in a healthy, focused mental state.

They even tried to shield the device from the effect of focused healing energy from a person and found nothing that would do so. The device wouldn't show any response of released electrons when electromagnetic energies were used on it to try and activate it. Electromagnetic energies are radiating energy waves like gamma rays, ultraviolet or infrared light, radio waves, visible light, x-rays, or high-voltage current. Tiller came to the conclusion that *humans emit a unique energy* that, when focused with intention, attention, and visualization, transfers information from the mind, which is capable of releasing negative electrons. This resulted in the awareness that intentions and thoughts may well be capable of releasing charges of energy which affect the charge balances of cell membranes, thus affecting the health of living cells.

Other research confirms that human intention, attention and imagery do have an effect on living systems. So what is science showing us? First of all, photons are massless, chargeless packets of "light" energy. When a photon of light goes into an atom, it gains energy. When a photon of light is released from an electron, which is inside an atom, it loses energy. Light energy comes from one ultimate life-giving source, God.

Light dispels the darkness in the body. Light adds energy to your systems. Light energy dispels the distorted energies in our life to cause healing. Have you been noticing how your thoughts can put light and life into yourself and others, or darken the light of life in you? This is why our intent, what we dwell upon, and what we observe are so important. We get results according to which energies we activate, reactivate, or keep activated because we were born generating energy.

Photons of Light; God's Energy

Remember the information about the tachyon? I believe that now you can see what I saw when I read about the tachyon discovery. When physicists released two photons of light from an atom, both spun far away in opposite directions. The physicists soon discovered that though they were thousands of miles apart, when they changed the spin of one photon, the spin of the other photon changed simultaneously as well.

The significance is this, since the photons (packets of light) are traveling away from each other at the speed of light, in order for the spin to change on the other proton, thousands of miles away, simultaneously indicates that the communication from one photon to the other had to happen faster than the speed of light. Not only that, but there had to be a higher energy connecting them, a third party energy, faster than the speed of light, that communicated information to both photons faster than the speed of light. Whose light energy do you think they found?

Strangely enough, every time they found evidence of that mysterious third party energy, it would disappear, only to reappear in unexpected places, violating their known laws of conservation of energy. This discovery was very disturbing—to say the least—to physicists and their minds which must know the what, where, when, and why of everything, so they can explain them logically. Things must be constant for them to explain them logically.

They can know where it is, and what it is, but not where it is and what it is at the same time.

Biophysicists call the subtle energy that humans possess, scalar or non-Hertzian energy. All known frequencies of energies are identified on a scale called the Hertz. Yet the subtle energies that humans possess exert an influence beyond the electromagnetic energy field, beyond known frequencies. What is the point? Just that God's energy is in us and they can't nail it down to define it or predict its behavior. Man was created in God's image and likeness. Hello! That is why physicists can't nail the Spirit down and why they don't like talking about it. They can't explain the Spirit of God in scientific terms. Their perception must fall within the realm of their five senses before they will believe the perception.

The Spirit of God isn't explained within the five senses dimension. It will never be explainable totally. Why? I think of one logical reason. If God revealed everything about Himself to us, then what we know, our enemy would also know. Besides, I don't think anything or anyone God created has the capacity to know all there is about God. This is why it is impossible to please God without faith. You have to believe He is beyond our capabilities of total understanding.

Isaiah says, "For as the heavens are higher than the earth, so are my ways higher than your ways, and my thoughts than your thoughts" (Isaiah 55:9). Many people take this verse the wrong way, thinking God is saying, "I am distant and you can't comprehend my thoughts." God is defining the difference between Himself and man, true, but notice that he does not say we cannot ask for some of those higher ways and thoughts, does it? In fact the verse before that says "For my thoughts are not your thoughts, neither are your ways my ways, saith the LORD" (Isaiah 55:8). It says our ways and thoughts are not His, but where does it say we can't ask Him for what His thoughts and ways are? We cannot get all of His thoughts and ways but we sure can get much more than we think or ask Him for.

Solomon had to have much more of God's thoughts and ways than any of us. In fact, He says in James 1:5 to ask "If any of you is deficient in wisdom, let him ask of the giving God [Who gives] to everyone liberally and ungrudgingly, without reproaching or fault-finding, and it will be given him" (AMP). He is a generous God, yet He won't give us what we will end up abusing Him or others with.

That's why science can't accept things of the spirit—neither the spirit of man, nor the Spirit of God. Yet what science discovers will prove God to be who the Word says He is.

Satan tried to deceive man to use the power of intention for evil. Look at what Genesis says:

And they said, Come, let us build us a city and a tower whose top reaches into the sky, and let us make a name for ourselves, lest we be scattered over the whole earth. And the Lord came down to see the city and the tower which the sons of men had built. And the Lord said, Behold, they are one people and they have all one language; and *this is only the beginning of what they will do, and now nothing they have imagined they can do, will be impossible for them.* (Genesis 11:4-6, AMP)

Satan united those people in thought for evil against God. It still shows the possibilities of intent when men set their focus on a goal. Man was told by God to multiply in the earth. When they decided to build a tower to the heavens of God, it was similar to the idea Satan had to make his position higher than God's.

God saw that their intent, sincere desire, and what they were observing. He saw they were focused on doing evil. God took action and confused their language. There used to be one universal language before that day.

What happened in the upper room would be an example of positive intent. They were all in one accord, with one focus, one spiritual language, in unity, forming one observation, one sincere desire, and one intention to seek God. And God delivered with a special visitation. (Read it in Acts 2.) Intent, sincere desire and observation creates a reality from what is not seen. It is calling forth those things that are not...as though they are.

Sowing and Reaping Law

When we create we must understand the law of sowing and reaping. Galatians 6:7 says, "Be not deceived; God is not mocked: for whatsoever a man soweth, that shall he also reap." God has plans for each of us. Jeremiah 29:11 says, "For I know the thoughts and plans that I have for you, says the Lord, thoughts and plans for welfare and peace and not for evil, to give you hope in your final outcome." Proverbs 19:21 says, "Many plans are in a man's mind, but it is the Lord's purpose for him that will stand." Proverbs 16:9 says,

"A man's mind plans his way but the Lord directs his steps and makes them sure."

Is your perception one that tells you to be careful what thoughts you focus on? Be careful what you *see* and what you *say*. You are painting on a word canvas and you are going to receive your future by your own words, starting with your thoughts. What you perceive, you receive. You are a transmitter and a receiver. The one with the perception has the reception. You really do create your future in your present.

Information comes in thoughts of information that hold possibilities that are flowing from your future, and that are waiting for you to take them captive to observe them. Then you call those thoughts, containing information that are not...as though they are. That is the next nanosecond you are doing something with. By you observing, focusing, and meditating, you cause things to be.

If by default you allow your thoughts to flow in at random, without paying them any attention, you are also, by default, allowing your present to repeat your past. Your *future becomes your past*. That is a big statement, so I will restate it: If you know your life to be nothing but more of the same old thing, it is because you are in your present, allowing your past to repeat itself. Your past is becoming your future. You are super glued to your past from bringing up your past failures. You will repeat them in your life.

The only way out of that wheel is to change your perceptions of belief, which changes your present future. We start by becoming aware of what we perceive. This is good news because we are the ones who, without a doubt, have the say-so over what happens in our life. It requires us doing something different. It requires our noticed and managed involvement, which is why fate doesn't exist without our involvement.

Even when you think you aren't doing something, you are. Things by default are still allowed to be, simply because you allow them to be. This is right where the kingdom of evil wants you to stay stuck—in unbelief, lacking knowledge, and far from the possibilities God packaged within you.

When we focus on God, He delights to show you who we really can become. Why, because you house a part of Him in you. Just as any parent watches their child and is proud to see her act like she acts, or look like she looks, God wants to see Himself through you. He wants, and needs you to express Him on earth. He created earth and then gave it to man. He told us to be fruitful and to multiply His goodness on earth. He didn't say He was going to dictate to us what to do, nor did He tell us to call upon Him for every change we want to make for His permission to implement it. No, He told man to take dominion and subdue it.

Yes, there is a period of time, by God's grace and mercy, when He answers prayer requests we make of Him. But there comes a time when every father wants his child to mature and take their adult position of responsibility and authority—to get involved with making things happen. He wants us to learn to be like Him through our spirit, soul, and body.

We have Power to Observe and Cause

Greater is He that is in you than he that is in this world. (1 John 4:4) Old things pass away and all things are made new by observing. Quantum physics and revolutionary science confirm that man has power to observe and cause. Old things passing away and all things being observed new is a truth. You have the capability to see where your tomorrow comes from.

David Van Koevering, in *Quantum Healing* summarizes this well:

> Popping a qwiff is looking out into the nanosecond ahead of you and seeing in that moment a reality that's in your desire and intent. It should be a God idea that you are reflecting in your consciousness. When you see what God sees, say what God has said in terms of promises, and what He has revealed for your future, your observation causes you to pop a qwiff. By that observation you cause that to flow into your future.
>
> John taught us in the Bible that we would see all things to come. When you see your destiny, a vision, or creative idea, your observation causes that idea or observation to flow into

your future. It is like the cosmos is waiting for you to pop a qwiff and to cause that to be your reality.

God is at the very core of everything created, holding it together. Satan hates man for the creative possibilities that are housed within him. Man holds packets of God's energy inside him. Are you seeing yourself for the possibilities you really carry inside of you? You better know how much your enemy is after your destruction. This is why it is important to seek knowledge. Note that Satan has no knowledge except what he has already seen and done. What knowledge he does have, he handles with expert skill to manipulate and distort it.

You have no idea what you carry on the inside of you, the God potential that only you have and no one else. Your potential holds possibilities that are unique to you—no one else has. Our thinking and acting is by default most of the time and that is keeping most of us captive and in bondage. When you see what God sees, and connect with His power and authority in you—your future potential changes. When you take captive your thoughts and consciousness, and align your heart with God, He restores and transforms you by His Holy Spirit.

Satan programs you to see what he sees thereby stealing from you what God wants you to see. He does this by twisting and injecting thoughts that are opposite to everything God's word shows us who we are and what we hold within us as future possibilities. He and his fallen angels do not want you to know that you really and truly can create the future God intends for you. Satan hates that he never could create. Do you see? Your future is in your present, now.

Chapter 16

Cells Store Memory

There is something important to remember about memory. Today it isn't difficult to believe that matter holds memory. We have CD's, computers, iPods', memory sticks, and so many other ways to hold and store memory. Information flows into these objects of matter and recalls it for many to hear.

It is known in the medical world that when people receive heart transplants, they acquire tastes for things they didn't enjoy before, or they display emotion differently. This is because the new heart holds memory. All cells hold memory.

Soldiers who have suffered serious injury to arms or legs, which result later in amputation, complain of feeling the same pain of the missing arm or leg. The other way the body can display a memory is when someone has been healed, yet later feels the same symptoms they felt when they were sick. The memory of that disease has been stored in the body's cells and the body remembers the symptoms, even though the person was healed. "Phantom pain" as doctors term it, can cause new problems in spite of the fact that the person no longer has a limb or was healed. Here is the science to explain why this happens.

Photons, bundles of energy in which light and other forms of electromagnetic radiation are emitted, go into matter and a negatively charged electron comes out.

This energy with light carries information in it. Those photons carry information into all matter. Many have said "If these walls could talk." Well let me tell you, they can. Keep reading I found this interesting when I learned of it. Everything you see with the eye is made up of atomic structures, including you. Information that is spoken or thought is moving through all atomic structures that are connected with each other. Everything is recorded in matter and will someday have the rewind/ play button on it pushed by God. And we think our words don't matter? Every spoken word carries images in it. Every spoken word and event done in the flesh is recorded, even in the stuff around us.

This is why Joshua says, "And Joshua said to all the people, See, *this stone shall be a witness against us, for it has heard all the words the Lord spoke to us;* so it shall be a witness against you, lest [afterward] you lie (pretend) and deny your God" (Joshua 24:27, AMP). Some of us never imagined how real that written word was.

Jesus also said in Luke 19:40, "And he answered and said unto them, I tell you that, if these should hold their peace, the stones would immediately cry out." Habakkuk 2:11 echoes this, "For the *stone shall cry out of the wall*, and the beam out of the timber shall answer it." Joshua sounded a frequency that canceled the frequencies of vibration of the walls at Jericho. Jesus' voice spoke through him.

This is how evil curses exist in people, places or things. (They also exist in and come through generational blood line.) DNA holds blueprints and blueprints are images (as shown earlier). Deuteronomy 30:19 says (my paraphrase), "I call heaven and earth to record this day against you, that I have set before you life and death, blessing and the cursing; therefore choose life, that you and your descendants may live." Your prayers in the name of Jesus are absolutely essential. They are the higher power that can cancel all lower powers of evil and former memory from matter. Jesus Christ's death and resurrection on the cross gives you authority in Him to do this. Did you just take a quantum leap? Be careful what you say.

Are you free from your past thoughts, words and actions? Did you ever consider that the way you speak and act could be coming from a generational curse that has followed you in the memory of cells that were passed on to you from your ancestors? Have you blessed your life or cursed it, unknowingly?

Jesus' blood flows in your veins when you became a believer in Him. Let me say it this way: Because Jesus shed His blood for our forgiveness; the frequencies of Jesus' blood transform your blood into "J.C. positive" substance. You can change everything. There is not one thing that has been recorded against you that you cannot change through Jesus, through the words that you or your ancestors spoke. You hold the power to remove and release curses in the name of Jesus.

How Sins are Washed Away

Let me paint with a sharp brush on your canvas just what I mean, so you can truly be set free. Jesus holds all things together, that means you too. Jesus' vibrations of energy have perfect, flawless waveform to them. When we repent for sin, that sin is washed by Jesus' Word because He gave His life, His blood, for us. This is what Psalm 51:2 says, "Wash me thoroughly from mine iniquity, and cleanse me from my sin." Acts 22:16 says, "And now why tarriest thou? arise, and be baptized, and wash away thy sins, calling on the name of the Lord." Revelation 1:5 says, "And from Jesus Christ, who is the faithful witness, and the first begotten of the dead, and the prince of the kings of the earth. Unto him that loved us, and washed us from our sins in his own blood."

What does the verse mean by "washed"? When we ask for forgiveness from our sins, Jesus takes the set of frequencies, those distorted energies that created the sin, and He immediately changes them to His sinless energies (frequencies of vibration) and so your sin no longer exists. The old vibrational distorted energy is no longer.

Does that mean you are now without sin? Not totally, for as long as we live in a cursed world, we don't see every single thing about ourselves. Not everything in us is conscious to our awareness so we can see it. We can never stop depending upon the Lord to reveal all things to us that are hidden.

In each act of repentance from the heart, you make the choice to ride His wave, align, harmonize, to be in sync, and to be in tune with Jesus' flawless, sinless waves of energy. You chose to be one with those waves and He changed the distortions. God cannot remember your sins because there is no substance there to remember. The former set of frequencies were transformed and replaced with the perfect frequencies of Jesus' who holds all things together. (See Hebrews 8:12, Hebrews 10:17, and Isaiah 43:2.)

I hope that provides a crystal clear picture for you to change your perception and belief about sin. It is never too late to repent for past sins. If you think you have committed too many for the Lord to forgive, you are listening to the lies of the enemy. He tricks you by bringing up your past and uses your lack of understanding of invisible energy against you, so you will curse yourself over the same things again.

To walk in His freedom comes with conditions. Conditions are what fallen human nature doesn't like. Man generally wants to do what he wants to do and expects no consequences for doing it. Even if that "doing" causes more sickness and pain to him or her than to obey God's word would. However, there are universal laws that needed to be put in place when God created this universe.

For example, you would not jump off the Empire State Building and expect there to be no consequences because of the law of gravity. Would you? No more can you continue to operate in default mode, without expecting to give the kingdom of sin legal rights to operate in you. This is what happened when man and woman fell in the garden. Obedience to God's word has always been the condition for receiving from the Lord. But obedience has been painted in our thinking like it is somehow lacking in pleasure. Obedience should be painted as a protection to keep our life healthy and whole.

Obedience is better than sacrifice. One either obeys and follows the kingdom of sin and its evil natures, or the Kingdom of God and His nature. We have free will to choose. This is where moving by faith applies. Romans 2:13 says, "For it is not merely hearing the Law [read] that makes one righteous before God, but it is the doers of the Law who will be held guiltless and acquitted and justified" (AMP). If you keep repeating the same evil behaviors, your distorted energies increase. The law of multiplication exists either for good or evil.

It is a problem when people are trying to fight a battle and don't even know who their enemy is. How does anyone fight for themselves when they don't really know who they are as a child of God, or who they have the potential to become? The answer is obvious: we can't so many don't. The war manual is the Word. It tells us in Isaiah 5:13, "Therefore my people are gone into captivity, because they have no knowledge." Hosea 4:6 says, "My people are destroyed for lack of knowledge: because thou hast rejected knowledge, I will also reject thee, that thou shalt be no priest to me: seeing thou hast forgotten the law of thy God, I will also forget thy children."

We are the ones who must take the initiative to fight for our rights both in the natural and spiritual realms. Many pray to God expecting Him to do everything for us. The sad part of that is many do not realize that He did it all for us already. He sent His son to pay a very high price for us to have authority in Him on earth. Now it is up to us to possess what is rightfully ours, by the use of the promises in His word. After all, the word of God is what the enemy uses to steal from us!

Maybe you didn't understand completely what God has given to you. Perhaps you still don't completely understand who you are in Him. I believe this is a new beginning for you. This is why I have laid a foundation for you to build upon for understanding how to live in health and wholeness with success in your life.

Chapter 17

Confessions Create Reality

I am about to explain as clearly as I can why speaking and what we speak is vital. What we speak determines what we receive into our life. This is more explainable and understandable than ever due to science discoveries about how energy moves. It shows once more that God had us covered right from the very beginning. We have no reason to be ignorant to the knowledge of how spiritual principles apply to our lives. This is how I discovered, in a small way, how to look at God and all He created and how that all affects me. Allow me to share my thoughts with you to cause transformation.

God made man, and then told man to multiply and replenish the earth. This is done by speaking His word throughout the earth. How? Through the mouth of mankind! The Lord needs His word to work both inside of us and outside of us in the earth.

We need certain things in our life in order to remain alive. Our body needs food to supply it with nutritional energy. Our brain (soul) needs the process of learning, through thinking, to exercise it. Our spirit needs food and the only source for that is the Word. Why? We are made from the words God spoke. Anyone who refuses to eat any of God's word cannot be helped by God. He needs His word to work within us. There are spiritual principles in place that the enemy knows and uses against man. These same spiritual principles are what God Himself cannot violate.

God is a giving God. God is a God of seed planting, allowing a season of time to pass before a harvest can take place. The type of seed you use will be measured back to you. You can't plant corn and expect pickles to grow. You must give out what you want to grow because it will be what you harvest. For example, God can't help people who sow seeds of bitterness toward another –who then pray, asking for a miracle from God to fix the *other* person so *they* will give them love and understanding. Was the seed that came out of your mouth love and understanding toward the other person?

There is a spiritual principal we all must know that I believe will be helpful.

No matter what your need is, whether physical, financial or whatever, it is vital to understand that it takes energy either to create a form of something, or to reform something. There is a multiplication of energy. The "type" of seed you use will be the fruit that is multiplied back to you.

For example, if you sow seeds of kind words generously, kindness is what will just as generously be returned to you. Sure there are always exceptions or tares that come up, but whatever the majority of the seed was that you planted, is what you will harvest.

This spiritual principal is found in Genesis 1:11, which says that man will get fruit after its own kind of seed. "And God said, Let the earth bring forth grass, the herb yielding seed, and the fruit tree yielding fruit after his kind, *whose seed is in itself*, upon the earth: and it was so."

In other words, depending upon what you want, you have to consider that things multiply according to their own seed. They only multiply when they are planted outside of "self" and in fertile soil. So how can you get anything from the inside of you to the outside? Through your words!

The measure, meaning the "type" and "amount" of measure you use, will be multiplied back to you accordingly. A measure has to be some type of substance, and quantity of a substance. I would like a half a glass of water. In this case the measure is half and water. Webster's dictionary defines measure as, "a *system or type* of measurement: liquid measure, and a definite or known *quantity* measured out: to drink a measure of wine."

According to the Word, you have to give that measure and that measure will be measured back to you. Look at Luke 6:38, "*Give, and [gifts] will be given to you*; good measure, pressed down, shaken together, and running over, will they pour into [the pouch formed by] the bosom [of your robe and used as a bag]. For with the measure you deal out [with *the measure you use* when you confer benefits on others], it *will be measured back to you*" (AMP).

Next, the word "giving" indicates a movement. You must place a giving energy, which moves the measure you use (a substance and amount of that substance or thing), causing that substance and amount of it, to come back to you pressed down, shaken together and running over into your bosom. Now bosom denotes and even is defined in Webster's as, "the breast, conceived of as the center of feelings or emotions. Our heart is in our bosom. That is where the measure we use comes back to us.

Hearing God and Stewarding What you Hear

One thing I want to interject here that I noticed in a new way from the word of God relating to how we hear Him speak to us and what we do with His word. Do we value His voice? Do we honor and place importance upon hearing from Him? If we are faithful with money for example, He gives us more. Then I would like to ask you, "If we are faithful with hearing His word, and are faithful with those words He gives us, would He give us more words?" Notice what Jesus said in Mark 4:24, "And he said unto them, Take heed *what* ye hear: with what measure ye mete, it shall be measured to you: and *unto you that hear shall more be given*. For he that hath, to him shall be given: and he that hath not, *from him shall be taken* even that which he hath." (AMP)

Jesus is talking about *what* you hear. This is used in reference to stewardship. But He is talking about hearing and hearing comes by words.

He is saying to us that we need to be a good steward with what we hear. If we are a good steward with what we hear, then we will hear more. But if not, He will take away what we have. Remember also that faith comes by hearing. Do you feel you don't have faith?

Check into what you are hearing and how you are listening and if you value the Word.

In Luke 8:18 it says almost the same thing except it says to take heed *how* you *listen*. "Be careful therefore *how* you *listen*. For *to him who has [spiritual knowledge] will more be given*; and from him who does not have [spiritual knowledge], even what he thinks and guesses and supposes that he has *will be taken away*." (AMP) You receive according to how you value *what you hear* and *how you listen* to the Word.

When God speaks to us we need to take notice of how we steward His word and make sure we receive His word into good soil. Having good soil would be to receive His word with meekness. See James 1:21b, "receive with meekness the engrafted word, which is able to save your souls." and with a humble tender heart as in Second Chronicles 34:27, "Because thine heart was tender, and thou didst humble thyself before God, when thou heardest his words against this place, and against the inhabitants thereof, and humbledst thyself before me, and didst rend thy clothes, and weep before me; I have even heard thee also, saith the LORD."

I never understood this like I do now having been in this sabbatical. What you are willing to invest in will bring you a blessing in return. To invest in the word of God by purchasing Bible based teachings through books, CD's, and classes is stewarding well what you are planting into your soil.

For example, we think nothing about spending ten to thirty dollars to see a movie and go out to eat, but if a book or CD set costs thirty dollars we may think it's to much to spend. Yet which is going to be the greater investment for a greater return of blessing into our lives? We spend our money on everything else and don't think twice about it, yet when we're asked to spend it on teachings, or books that would bring the word of God into us, we say, we can't afford it. We have to begin to think about investing into ourselves and our children, basing it on what is going to yield the greater return from our investment for our lives.

Speaking what we Hear

Why is speaking the Word so important to acquire what you really want from God? God has to have His word to work with. His Word is on the inside of you. We produce because of a seed that has been planted, waiting a certain time for growth and then we can harvest. This is why it is important to value the Word. How do you think we plant what life gives us? Whatever we plant comes straight out of our mouths. This is why it is said that the tongue is the most unruly member of the body in James 4: 8, "But the tongue can no man tame; it is an unruly evil, full of deadly poison."

Too often, we speak things that are negative and those are the words that are worked with in the spiritual realm. We see what we say and say what we see. *If we want to change what we say, then we must change what we see.* We must realize that we have the blessings of God's word to cause positive breakthroughs in our lives.

We have some positive things we can do that work the Word to our benefit. In Job 22:28 it talks about decreeing a thing in order to establish it. We overcome by the spirit of prophecy, which is the testimony of Jesus. To testify of what Jesus has done in your life is to speak out His glory for others to see (you paint with your words on a canvas in their minds) and it encourages them to want what you painted for them. (See Revelation 19: 10.) It also plants hope in them which is the key ingredient to faith.

Most of the time, without realizing it, we testify of our problems and that isn't shining any of the Lord's light from inside you to the outside for others to receive. Those words are the words the enemy is looking to pick up to harvest. The enemy needs those negative words you plant outside of yourself to harvest his desires. If you speak them you can cancel them by speaking the blood of Jesus over them commanding them to be rendered void. Are you seeing that it works the same from either direction—the enemy or God?

God needs our words to work with in this earth realm, but so does Satan. Why, because this planet was given to man by God. Satan loves to counterfeit godly spiritual principals and uses laws to produce what he wants because he thinks he is god. Too many people don't even realize that this is a fixed law of God. What enters this atmosphere of earth must come through man because it was created and given to us to take dominion over and to subdue. The way things produce and come into existence in earth is through every spoken word man speaks out and acts upon.

Faith is the substance of things hoped for and the evidence of what you don't see. Be careful of what you hope for as it works with invisible motion to show up. Unfortunately, you may not like the results you have been creating with your faith. Now is the time to become aware and change your thoughts. Faith works invisibly and substance will produce physically at some point in time.

Faith is invisible motions of energy (and we know all energy originates from God). As with all energy, the enemy works to distort good energy. Faith works to produce what isn't seen at first, but will eventually show up in the physical world. Think about what shows up when you lose hope: despair, depression, thoughts of suicide, and others. God says His people perish for lack of knowledge (or for no knowledge).

Change What You Confess

Now let's become aware of how to change this for the good. Confession is a spiritual principal. Confessing is affirming and speaking something we believe. This is mostly referenced as confessing our sins to one another. There is more to its meaning. If we spend more time being "sin conscious" than we do being "blessing conscious," we are asking for trouble. When we focus on our sins we are resonating with negative, toxic thoughts, continuing in harmony with what brings bad into our lives. The answer is to quickly repent and move back into positive controls.

Prophet, Kim Clement puts it like this: "Sin removes the ability to see the greatness of God in you." Sin blinds you. When you have a sin consciousness all the time, you see your "self" instead of seeing God in you. What you are conscious of is what you will see, both in and outside of you in others. The more you are conscious of evil, the more evil you will see in others.

The opposite is true as well: the more you are conscious of good that is what you will see in others and receive back from others. If all you see is sin in yourself; that is all you will see in others. Not only that, but it will be what you negatively focus on as well, which will not prohibit the growth of healthy trees in your brain. When you do this, you keep your negative control system activated too much of the time. That will not put you back on top and will keep your positive control system turned off.

Therefore, that is why we need to repent quickly and move into thinking thoughts from the positive control system within. This is what I believe King David had going for him. After he sinned, he didn't waste a lot of time before turning his thoughts back to God and asking for forgiveness. This could be what caused God to describe David as a man after His own heart.

God is looking for obedience. It doesn't matter how much sin you have been polluted with, He just wants you to keep giving your heart back to Him, by realizing the wrong you did and acknowledging it to Him. He will always continue to help you to overcome. Why? He IS love and He knows how His enemy Satan deceives all of His sons and daughters. The battle is God's and His Word has numerous promises, telling us that He will always protect us—with the condition that we stay connected to Him.

Mark 11:23 says, "whosoever shall SAY unto this mountain, Be thou removed, and be thou cast into the sea; and shall not doubt in his heart, but shall believe those things which he SAITH shall come to pass; he shall have whatsoever he SAITH."

You can always tell if a person's beliefs are positive or negative by what he/she speaks. If his confession is wrong, his believing is wrong. When believing is wrong, it is because his thoughts are wrong. Always, when thinking is wrong, it is because the mind needs renewing by the Word of God.

The Enemy applies Spiritual Laws to your Confessing

Hold on to the thought I gave you earlier that our enemy counterfeits everything and uses spiritual principals and laws to do what he does. (I will come back to that thought in a minute.)

First, notice what God tells us. Signs don't follow the individual, they follow the Word. Signs are confirming what the spoken Word has said. Signs are things that happen for us to see. I am making two solid points here.

First, we have to give the Lord His Word, spoken by us, for Him to be able to work with something. (We learned how that worked a few pages back.) Then that Word has to be confessed by us to work outside of us as well as in us. That is the process of faith.

Second, no matter what word we confess by speaking it, it has this spiritual principal to follow. Confessing is affirming something we believe out loud, for the invisible energies of God to work with. The substance of what is hoped for gets formed invisibly to appear physically. Now watch what happens.

In Mark 16, we are told that the Holy Spirit and the Father work only in conjunction with the Word. We must give them the Word in us to work with it in the earth; it's our domain. Mark 16:15-20 says:

> And he said unto them, Go ye into all the world, and preach the gospel to every creature. He that believeth and is baptized shall be saved; but he that believeth not shall be damned. And these signs shall follow them that believe; In my name shall they cast out devils; they shall speak with new tongues; They shall take up serpents; and if they drink any deadly thing, it shall not hurt them; they shall lay hands on the sick, and they shall recover. So then after the Lord had spoken unto them, he was received up into heaven, and sat on the right hand of God. And they went forth, and preached every where, the *Lord working with them, and confirming the word with signs following.* (Mark 16:15-20)

Notice in this context the Lord confirmed the gospel Word that they "spoke." Because that is how anything enters this atmosphere on earth. Notice that He didn't do a thing until they spoke the Word. When the Word is confessed, the signs will take care of themselves.

Inadvertently, even when speaking the Word, we can get tradition and unbelief mixed in with it. The important point is in the believing, and thinking in line with God's word, which is confessing: saying, affirming, and witnessing to what His word says that makes the difference. Your motive and intent are important. The greater clarity you speak with, the greater the signs that will follow what you say.

Now back to what I said earlier. The enemy counterfeits everything of God in the spirit realm. He takes his negative word you agree to speak and applies a spiritual principal of "whatsoever ye saith, ye shall believe, ye shall have." He then works those words of your confession and signs appear that follow what you say. The enemy applies spiritual laws to your confessing.

What signs are following your words? We are ignorant of his devices, ways, and means. He is a legalist: he takes God's principals and laws and works them for his evil intentions. The real trickery is that he has taught us to blame God for every bit of what is wrong about our lives because we are blinded to the truth by his dastardly thinking.

Faith's Confessions Create Realities

There is no faith without confession. Confession is the way for faith to express itself. Faith is by your spirit. You won't confess anything without having the faith to believe it. What you are confessing is the substance you are hoping for by faith to show up in your life. What you confess is coming from what you believe in your heart. Faith comes out of either your positive or negative control system by your confessions. Faith then grows with your confession. (your faith incubates, more on this in the chapter on Incubating Faith) The more you confess a thing, the more you will produce what you confess. If you say "I cannot," it is because you believe you cannot and your "I cannot" will be what you see, because you confessed what you believe.

If you really become aware of how what you say makes all the difference inside and outside of you, you can get busy and seriously change things about your life. You will turn yourself into being more than a conqueror and your life to one of victory. You can never be a conqueror until you think like one and confess like a conqueror.

We all say what we believe in our heart and if you wait to become whatever you are expecting to see, before you speak what you don't see in your present, you are sadly mistaken to think you will ever see it. It doesn't work that way because God put faith as the activation switch to create what you want. It is impossible to please Him without faith. Can you see why? We are wired to create by faith like He does.

Sadly, many Christian don't understand how the enemy is allowed to work in their lives and most seem to believe that their prayers don't even work. He tells us to believe what He says about Him, and us, in the Bible. If we don't, we are calling Him a liar. That separates us from Him and we are unable to create with Him. It puts us in agreement (agreement is whom our energy is in harmonize with) with our enemy to create what he gets us to see. God cannot answer the opposite of what you believe; it would make Him a liar to His own word and put Him in harmony with the devil. He would have to apologize for His own Son's death on the cross.

Wrong confession is a confession of defeat. If you talk about how the devil is keeping you from success, keeping you sick, or keeping you weak, it "is" keeping you weak or sick or unsuccessful — and that glorifies him. That is talking "about" your mountain when you must talk "to" your mountains to move them out of the way.

Examine things this way; ask yourself what control system you have activated when you think about the thing, and take a look at what you say. You can realize which switch you have turned on by examining your thoughts and listening to what you say. If the words you hear in your mind are negative, you know your positive control system is turned off and chances are your words coincide with the thoughts.

You don't have to identify the source from where those negative thoughts came, unless the Holy Spirit reveals that to you. If He does, it will be for one purpose only, so you can ask His forgiveness for agreeing with them. Ask Him to help you think the opposite of those thoughts. Wash yourself with His Word (a spiritual bath you might say). That is the way to heal yourself from them. Then engage your positive thoughts and emotions. That will fill you with energies of light. The word brings His glorious light into you, that light is what heals your wounds from life.

The seeds of energy you use be they positive or negative are what you cause to become. Positive thought energy, once spoken, creates living, breathing, fruitful harvests that multiply. Spoken negative thought energy tears down, distorts, kills, steals, and destroys what could have been full of life—multiplying it unto death. Whichever energy you use most consistently, the more you will see happen from what the energy has the ability to do. Don't be double-minded. Positive creates life, negative destroys to kill. The seed of invisible energy brings our harvest of physical matter. Satan takes dominion over you with negative energy production if you agree. God's positive energy system overrides Satan's if you will be in tune with Him.

In Mark 11:22, Jesus tells us to have faith in God, "And Jesus answering saith unto them, Have faith in God." He tells us that; knowing that we can have devil faith that destroys us. In other words, have faith in God, not devil faith. It is impossible to please God without faith. Why? You can also have faith in the devil without realizing what you are confessing. It is according to what you believe and confess.

Mark 11:23-24 says, "For verily I say unto you, That whosoever shall say unto this mountain, Be thou removed, and be thou cast into the sea; and shall not doubt in his heart, but shall BELIEVE that those things which he SAITH shall come to pass; he shall have whatsoever he SAITH." Therefore I say unto you, What things soever ye desire, when ye pray, believe that ye receive them, and ye shall have them."

He wants you to have faith that comes by hearing and hearing by the word of God—not hearing the twisted words of Satan. Realize that Satan takes the Word of God and rewords it into doubt and unbelief to try to draw you into believing against God, to separate you from Him. It is God's word he works with to twist into lies. *He doesn't even write his own material.* He copies and rearranges the words from God and speaks to us a different meaning than the original text. Exactly the same thing he originally did in the mind of Eve in the Garden of Eden. It's time we *wake up and sue Satan for copyright infringement against your written will and trust from Jesus Christ, as a son or daughter of the Lord.*

Whatever you confess has dominion over you. You must practice God's word for it to work. You will continue with problems when you confess you are weak or sick or have pain. It is working negative energy throughout your physical operating system. This is why some receive healing in a faith energized atmosphere and go home to lose it. Bringing up your past failures or mistakes is harmonizing with negative energy and will cost you your faith in the Word. Don't spend your time there; it only gets you more of the same energy. You build those thoughts into your consciousness, demolish tree branches, and will eventually kill your root system in the heart.

Ask yourself one question when you are deciding on challenging thoughts: "What does God say about this?" God will never give you a negative prognosis about any situation. He wants only that which is good in gifts to give us. Matthew 7:11 says, "If ye then, being evil, know how to give good gifts unto your children, how much more shall your Father which is in heaven give good things to them that ask him?" The *condition* however is that you change your beliefs to match what He says.

No matter how long you pray or have anyone else pray for you, if you act and think against what the Word says about your condition or circumstances, the Word can't work for you. When you harmonize with it by activating and keep active your positive control system, the energy natures of the Word will work for you and in you. You have to give God that word to work with on your behalf.

Prophesying over Yourself

We are to prophesy over our "self" for this reason. You must say what we don't see in the natural in order to prophesy. To prophesy is to make inspired declarations of what is to come—the words given to cause invisible motion. Everything is coming to pass as prophesied in the word of God.

Paul tells us to prophesy in 1 Corinthians 14:1 saying to grow spiritual gifts but especially prophecy. "*Eagerly pursue* and seek to acquire [this] love [make it your aim, your great quest]; and earnestly desire and cultivate the spiritual endowments (gifts), especially that you may prophesy ([a]interpret the divine will and purpose in inspired preaching and teaching)" (AMP).

Revelation 19:10 tells us that the spirit of prophecy is the testimony of Jesus in your life. In other words, what you speak that the

Lord has done in your life is a spoken word of prophecy for anyone else who hears those words and applies them to their life. This is another illustration given to us to understand how the word of the Lord works on our behalf to give us life and life more abundantly. Hope is built in us when we hear testimonies of what the Lord has done in someone else's life.

Robert Morris, senior pastor of Gateway Church, in a sermon spoke about the spiritual meaning of water being likened to the Word. Psalm 1:1-3 says, "Blessed is the man that walketh not in the counsel of the ungodly, nor standeth in the way of sinners, nor sitteth in the seat of the scornful. But his delight is in the law of the LORD; and in his law doth he meditate day and night. And *he shall be like a tree planted by the rivers of water,* that bringeth forth his fruit in his season; his leaf also shall not wither; and *whatsoever he doeth shall prosper."*

You prosper with negative or positive prosperity, and here is why: Water represents words in the Bible. Proverbs 18:4 tells us: "The *words of a man's mouth are as deep waters*, and the wellspring of wisdom as a flowing brook." The war with your enemy is *a war of words*. Satan's twisted words against God's word of truth. This battle happens every day of our lives here on earth. But!

Pay attention to that BUT!

We have been given the word of God to overcome the enemy but we must believe and agree and speak them forth into this atmosphere we live in to bring stuff to pass. God's word is the most powerful energy when applied through a believer with authority against Satan and his kingdom. Satan has no energy of his own that he can pull out of a hat to use against God. He uses what comes from God and distorts all of it. There is no way Satan's energy is more powerful than the energy of God. Put another way, there is no way that the words of the enemy are more powerful than the words of God. God is the original source for all power. How we word things is how we throw energy around. Be careful what you speak.

Look at Revelation 12:9-11:

And the great dragon was cast out, that old serpent, called the Devil, and Satan, which deceiveth the whole world: he was cast out into the earth, and his angels were cast out with him. And I *heard a loud voice saying* in heaven, Now is come salvation, and strength, and the kingdom of our God, and the power of his Christ: for *the accuser of our brethren is cast down*, which accused them before our God day and night. And *they overcame him by the blood of the Lamb, and by the word of their testimony;* and they loved not their lives unto the death.

This tells us that the serpent is Satan, which is the same serpent who came to Eve in the Garden of Eden, who uses words to produce our destruction.

Satan wants to *flood* us. Now what do I mean by flood? Go to verse 15 of Revelation 12, "And the serpent *cast out of his mouth water as a flood* after the woman, that he might cause her to be carried away of the flood." The woman represents the body of Christ, or all believers. Satan spewed out of his mouth water (*words*) as a flood against the believers of Christ. Everyday Satan is coming against us with a flood of words that disagree with the word of God. Are you still thinking that your words don't really matter? I pray the eyes of your understanding be enlightened now, in Jesus name. (Ephesians 1:18)

Men and Women's Minds are Like a Garden

This is the same method he used in the Garden of Eden to speak to Eve. Nothing has changed in Satan's method. Why because it is working for him. In fact, do you want to know where the Garden of Eden is? It's inside of you! Men and women's minds are likened unto a garden. We are the master gardeners of our soul.

The mind has trees with branches that were designed to bear fruit that have a trunk that grows up from the roots that are in our heart. Just as a gardener cultivates and tends to his garden, keeping it free from weeds to grow fruit-bearing plants, so we tend the garden of our minds, weeding out the wrong and impure toxic thoughts, so as to cultivate life-producing thoughts that bear fruit in the branches of our trees. If no useful seeds are planted in our gardens, then useless weeds and tares will continue to multiply, producing more of their own kind. Matthew 13:25 says, "But while men slept, his enemy came and sowed tares among the wheat, and went his way."

Every word of seed sown that is allowed coming into the mind and taking root in the heart produces after its own kind. Good words bear good fruit, bad words bear bad fruit—everything produces after its own type of seed.

Have you ever experienced a flood of words coming into you that told you negative things? Do you know where they are coming from? Matthew 7:24-25 tells us this very same thing about Satan being a flood, but also tells us how to save ourselves.

> Therefore whosoever heareth these sayings of mine, and doeth them, I will liken him unto a wise man, which built his house upon a rock: (Jesus, the word of God is the rock) And the rain descended, and the floods came (the flood are words from Satan), and the winds blew, and beat upon that house (the house is you); and it fell not: for it was founded upon a rock. (Jesus the word of God). (Author Notations)

Now the problem, as we already should know, is if we agree with the flood of words from the enemy. Proverbs 6:2 says, "Thou art *snared with the words of thy mouth*, thou art *taken with the words of thy mouth."* We end up in bondage with our own words.

The Lord never leaves us hanging without telling us what to do. Here is the good news, Isaiah 59:19, "When the enemy shall come in like a flood, the Spirit of the LORD shall lift up a standard against him." But here is the thing; the standard is the word of God. You must use the truth to stand against the enemy's lies. You have to use the Word as a weapon against his words. That requires confession.

Satan comes against us with *famine*. What do I mean? He doesn't want you to know that it is him talking to you, but tries instead to make you think it is you talking. He talks to you in the first person to make what he says sound like it is you talking to yourself. It would be too obvious that it was him talking if he came to you and said, "Look what you just did! Now you are never going to get ahead!" No. He says it just like it's you talking, "I am so stupid, look what

I just did, I will never get ahead." He knows the word of God is the only thing that has power over him.

Bread and water represent the word of the Lord for us to eat and drink daily and Satan causes a famine of the Word in you. He tries to steal the Word. Mark 4:15 says, "And these are they by the way side, where the word is sown; but when they have heard, *Satan cometh immediately, and taketh away the word that was sown in their hearts.*" Why? Because he knows that the Word is the seed planted in the hearts of man and that seed will take root and bear fruit unless he steals it, (especially if we've watered the seed with more of God's word). That is why he focuses relentlessly on keeping us out of the word of God. We find out who we are and our purpose in life by reading the word of God. And that purpose certainly isn't to allow Satan to work his plan, but rather to defeat him in our lives.

Now you need not feel discouraged because all answers you need to overcome anything in this life are found in the word of God. The Lord wants to fill us with His river of living waters. See that here in Revelation 22:1, "And he shewed me a *pure river of water of life,* clear as crystal, proceeding out of the throne of God and of the Lamb." This is saying that the water (words of life) are pure and proceed out of the throne of God. Where do they go? Into our hearts because we already established that is where they go when we learned that it is the place Satan comes to steal them from us.

But look at what Revelation 22:17 says: "And the Spirit and the bride say, Come. And let him that heareth say, Come. And let him that is thirsty come. And whosoever will, let him take the water of life freely." Whoever desires to take the water of life (the Word of God) receives freely. Notice again where this free word is promised to us by God. Revelation 21:6 says, "And he said unto me, It is done. I am Alpha and Omega, the beginning and the end. I will give unto him that is athirst of the fountain of the water of life freely."

The enemy floods us with negative words that lie, but God has given us a fountain of the water of life. This fountain is on the inside of us. John 4:14 says, "But whoever takes a drink of the water (the word of God) that I will give him shall never, no never, be thirsty any more. But the water (Word) that I will give him shall become a spring of water welling up (flowing, bubbling) [continually] within him unto (into, for) eternal life" (AMP, Author Notations). Sounds to me like a fountain inside of us. We think it is on the outside for us to look for. It all is on the inside of us.

Water Conducts Energy & You are 70% Water

Now let me plant this thought in you. The body is seventy percent water. You need to take a spiritual bath with the Word, if not, the enemy causes your water to literally stagnate or become polluted in your body. How does an operating system function in pollution? It soon fills with sewage.

In Ephesians 5:26 it talks about the washing of water by the Word. The water is the Word of life. When you focus on what it is saying and hear it, especially speaking it from your own mouth, it washes away the stain of sin on the inside of you. Psalm 51:2 says, *"Wash me thoroughly from mine iniquity,* and *cleanse me from my sin."* Acts 22:16 says, "And now why tarriest thou? arise, and be baptized, and *wash away thy sins,* calling on the name of the Lord." By calling on the word of God, we are given a spiritual cleansing bath.

Don't you think the enemy would want to stop this? After all, that washing erases the work he has already done in us. Don't think he gives up at that point. He goes right back to "flooding" you with his words, and if you don't know what is happening, he starts to pollute you again.

We Need a Spiritual Bath Daily

When you accept Jesus into your heart and are "born again" or "become saved," your spirit is _justified_ by the shed _blood_ of Jesus Christ. Justified means to be declared innocent or guiltless, absolved, acquitted, to be just as if you had never sinned. Revelation 1:5 says, "Unto him that loved us, and *washed us from our sins in his own blood."* Your spirit is made whole and you become a new creation. Your spirit is then seated in heavenly places with Christ Jesus, by grace. This happens immediately to your spirit when you accept Jesus into your heart, by the washing in the blood of Christ.

However, we are _sanctified_ by the _Word_. There is a difference between being justified by the blood of Christ and being sanctified by the Word. Justification happens immediately when you are born again; your spirit is cleansed by the blood of Christ. Sanctification is a long-term process. You are sanctified by the washing of the water of the Word. This washing is what is necessary for your soul to be made whole. Whereas your spirit becomes instantly whole by the blood, your soul is being made whole by the Word washing your soul clean (over time). This is the next step after you are born again, to be aware that you need a daily bath of the Word to grow in the Lord.

This is why, after months and years after being saved, people feel condemned by the enemy. They don't understand that their souls need to wash in the word of God in order to defeat the attacks from the enemy in their day to day lives. This is why the instructions found in the manual of the Bible are waters (words) of life to your very existence and survival in this cursed world system. This is why even Christians struggle so much with impure thoughts, they don't wash their mind with the word of God. The enemy loves to keep you dirty and in the dark. He puts diseases on you and steals the life from you on the inside. He takes advantage of you in the dark.

This is why the Word says we should not be of this world but must be transformed by the renewing of our mind. This is why the word of God is so necessary for our minds to bathe in every day. Do you think your enemy and his kingdom of devils takes a day off? Do you think they go on vacation for a week? Do you think he moved to another country? Absolutely not! He is the prince of the power of the air. That is the same air we have to breathe, every moment of every day while we live here on earth.

So get in the river every day!

Do you want to make a noticeable change in your life from whatever is happening, or not happening for you? Then let's start a program that is sure to make a transformation in your life, for sure. Oh you might ask me how I can be so sure of myself. I am sure, because the Word tells me so. I will not call the word of God a liar. That is how I am so sure that there is nothing impossible for anyone to transform in their life. Here is the thing; you have to want to be transformed because no one else can make that decision for you but you. And no one can do what needs to be done but you. That is why nobody else can change another person. God gave dominion to mankind over everything but one—other people. Jump in and start taking a daily bath in His word!

That is how important the Word is. Before we get into what you can do about this revelation to change your life, I have to illustrate to you how important to your survival everything is that comes out of your mouth.

Robert Morris had this to say about the breath of God. Now if you are going to use the word of God to make a change, it would be good for you to know that the word is literally God's breath. How long can you go without food? How long could you go without water? Now how long do you think you can live without oxygen? Let's see the evidence of that.

Second Timothy 3:16 says that all Scripture is God-breathed. The Scriptures are the very breath of God. Ezekiel 37 speaks about the valley of dry bones. Look at what it says in verses 5-6 and 8-10. There was no breath in the bones. In this scripture, the breath of God transforms a valley of dry bones into an army.

The breath of God *brings understanding* to us. Job 32:8 says, "But there is [a vital force] a spirit [of intelligence] in man, and the breath of the Almighty gives men understanding" (AMP). Ezekiel 37:4 says, "Again He said to me, Prophesy to these bones and say to them, O you dry bones, hear the word of the Lord" (AMP). And what is the breath of God? God's word! Who opens our understanding? Let's look at Luke 24:45, "Then opened he their understanding, that they might understand the Scriptures," The word of the Lord opens our understanding.

Without breath or oxygen, we panic—we don't think straight. We can't think straight without understanding what in the world is happening to us. How do we try to understand? More often than not, by talking to everyone around us that we possibly can. How well has that worked for any of us? Psalm 33:6 says, "By the word of the LORD were the heavens made; and all the host of them by the *breath of his mouth.*"

Yet we think we can do all things by ourselves or with the help of other people. We must consider where to look for our answers and to get our direction.

Look at Genesis 1:3. God said that He spoke light and it became. When He spoke it, it happened. The Word goes beyond just words. Isaiah 55:11 says, "So shall My word be that goes forth from My mouth; It shall not return to Me void, But it shall accomplish what I please, And it shall prosper in the thing for which I sent it."

What area of your life needs to come into alignment and order? The breath of God gives us strength for all areas. In Psalms we find more confirmation of this truth. Psalms 18:15-17 says, "Then the channels of waters were seen, and the foundations of the world were discovered at thy rebuke, O LORD, at the blast of the breath of thy nostrils. He sent from above, he took me, he drew me out of many waters.(water represents words) He delivered me from my strong enemy, and from them which hated me: for they were too strong for me." (Author Nation)

Another example of the breath of God can be found in Exodus:

And with *the blast of thy nostrils* the waters were gathered together, the floods stood upright as an heap, and the depths were congealed in the heart of the sea. The enemy said, I will pursue, I will overtake, I will divide the spoil; my lust shall be satisfied upon them; I will draw my sword, my hand shall destroy them. Thou didst blow with thy wind, the sea covered them: they sank as lead in the mighty waters. (Exodus 15:8-10)

John 20:22 says, "And when he had said this, *he breathed on them*, and saith unto them, Receive ye the Holy Ghost." This is why the Word says that we shall receive power when the Holy Spirit comes upon us.

Most importantly, *His breath gives us life.* Ezekiel 37:10 speaks again of the bones coming together and being given life when the breath of God's Word spoke them to life. "So I prophesied as he commanded me, and the *breath came into them, and they lived,* and stood up upon their feet, an exceeding great army."

Second Peter 1:20-21 says they spoke the word of God. When you speak, the breath of God is released into your situation to change it. Not your words, but His words.

Proverbs 4:20-22 tells how important the spoken word is: "My son, *attend to my words;* incline thine ear unto my sayings. Let them not depart from thine eyes; keep them in the midst of thine heart. *For they are life unto those that find them, and health to all their flesh."* The Lord is telling us that His words are life and health to all of our flesh. Are you beginning to see what is missing in your life?

God's Breath is His Voice

One last thing I want you to really see in relationship to the breath of God has the most to do with you personally. Go to Genesis 2 to understand what God really did when He created you and me. Talking about Adam, Genesis 2:7 says, "And the LORD God formed man of the dust of the ground, and <u>breathed into his nostrils the breath of life</u>; and man became a living soul." Job speaks about where he came from in Job 33:4, "The spirit of God hath made me, and the breath of the Almighty hath given me life." What brought Adam to life? The very breath of God did. But wait, that isn't the only thing you should realize from this.

How was and is everything created by God? He spoke it into existence, right? His voice creates all things. Now let me ask, what did He put into man when He breathed into His nostrils? He put His voice into him. In the original Hebrew of the Torah, that word "breath" is "voice." His voice is inside you.

You have the full capability to speak to your mountains and cause them to be moved. You have the full capacity to speak with the voice of God to your enemy. Now ask yourself, why would Satan be so interested in twisting the word of God in your head? Don't you think it would be because of the potential you have for taking the word of the Lord and changing your life with it?

If you would speak life to your world from the Word, which comes from an accurate belief in who you were created to be by the Word, which comes from a renewing of the mind from the Word, which comes from a change of heart to become congruent with your mind, which all comes back to the beginning where you take captive every thought you choose to dwell upon on a daily basis and consider what you say because what you believe in your heart is what you say. Then you can turn your world around in ways beyond your current belief. You create all the time. *It all starts with your thoughts and what you say.*

This is why God has told us to bring heaven to earth, because we carry the voice of God in us. We are hooked up and have a connection that is a powerful threat to Satan and his kingdom.

Chapter 18

Faith is Incubated

*F*aith demands to be fulfilled, either way, for good or for bad. It is the invisible motion of energies from which things get created. The Word says to work faith through love. God is love energy. God is saying to work our faith with love energies, to work our faith in Him. Galatians 5:6, "For [if we are] in Christ Jesus, neither circumcision nor uncircumcision counts for anything, but only faith activated and energized and expressed and working through love." (AMP) The verses before Proverbs 8: 21 speak of many good things that come from the Lord but notice what verse 21 says, "That I may cause those that love me *to inherit substance*; and I will fill their treasures." What substance is faith?

Faith is a substance of something we hope for; the substances are in the pictures you look at with focused intent, believing they will come to pass. This defines hope. How are those images a substance? Let's back up to understand that: 1) each thought is a packet of energy; 2) every substance is made up of energy; 3) energy originates with thought. Many thoughts put together are many frequencies that are capable of forming physical images. These all had their beginnings with thought images on the inside of someone.

Bear with me for a one paragraph side note. Think about what was just explained. Have you ever wondered why God gets so upset when people worship idols? For example, consider the golden calf the Israelite's built when they got tired of waiting for Moses to come down from the mountain and God was angered and judged them. He was angry because He knows that internal thoughts are images from the garden of our heart that manifest physically to reveal either the kingdom of darkness or the Kingdom of God. Those physical realities God knows will manifest both in our physical bodies and in our physical world. He knows well how his enemy Satan operates through His offspring. It is likely the idol worshiper does not realize what is happening inside of them. This is why God sent us His Word through Jesus and the Bible, so we will understand His kingdom and so He will be able to protect us.

Now back to the faith and hope explanative. One can become hopeless for anything good to happen in one's life, and therefore nothing good will happen. Why? Somewhere along the way you came to believe that what life holds for you are all bad things. In fact, one can hope to die and then make it happen.

Our spirit was created to create and resolve problems. This is the way mankind operates. In fact, the Bible says that God made man in His own image and likeness. The word "likeness" in the Hebrew means to "operate like." We operate like God in the fact that we co-create things. Anyone, at any time, can always hope and get something good to happen.

Hope is a Substance of Energy

Let's put it this way, hope is a substance which is a certain energy that vibrates at a certain frequency, just as desire, trust and belief have their own frequencies of energy. Positive energies from God can comingle with positive energies because they harmonize with each other. The opposite is also true of negative energies. Fear, doubt, unbelief, and distrust are also energies with vibrations of frequencies. Negative energy comingles with like negative energy because the vibrations are similar and harmonize with each other when put together. Positive energy cancels out negative energy and vice versa.

To present a better picture of this, let me add that positive energy holds light, while negative energy has no light and is dark. When you turn on a light in a dark room, where does the darkness go? It is utterly removed and canceled out. Positive energy of light also moves faster than negative energy.

Everything comes from God; all things are made up of energy and their source for existence is the original Creator. The Word says Jesus holds all things together. That is true because he is the Word of God. We also know God is omnipresent, meaning He is everywhere at all times. We can understand how this is possible, knowing that everything that exists is made up of energy. A negative form of energy causes a positive energy form to become distorted from its original vibration properties—it changes vibration. Because God is always present everywhere, there is always positive energy available to harmonize with—always there to create good in our lives.

God Himself acted by faith when He created the entire universe and all that is within it, including mankind. It is impossible to please God without the action of faith. Faith always starts out in the invisible realm. Once you see something, you no longer need to hope for it. Hope disappears when it has become physical for us to see with our natural eyes. Our continual thinking of the thoughts we have in the hope of something materializing is the action of comingling the like energy of what you are seeing while you hope for it.

Genesis 1:2 says, "the Spirit of God was moving (hovering, brooding) over the face of the waters" (AMP). That word "moving" means "to brood over." Brood is defined as "the action of dwelling on a subject, or to meditate with continued persistence." Just as God brooded over the earth as He gave it form, so the thoughts, images of what you see, are inside you, incubating until a birth takes place. You are an incubator, as you will discover.

How can Satan create when he has no intrinsic creative ability? He needs our incubators to get his evil thoughts to become reality on earth. He can only re-create energy which comes from God by distorting it. Faith, the action that takes place with thoughts in our incubator, can work the same when we meditate on positive or negative thoughts. Either way, by faith we produce things. If negative fear is incubating in you, and thus you have faith in those thoughts, you can cause them to come to pass.

The kingdom of darkness will try to get you to meditate with morbid persistence on doubt and unbelief, knowing that when those images reach your heart, they will cancel out the positive thoughts you had been incubating for your good. You can have continued persistence on either positive thoughts or negative thoughts. Both cause something to come into reality in the physical.

If you recognize what the enemy is doing in your mind, you must immediately take those thoughts of doubt and unbelief out of your mind and ignore them with continued persistence. Stay focused on the good pictures in your heart and you shall have what you see in due time. Remember that God is the only one with the big picture. Everything we hope for fits into the big picture in proper time.

Say What You See

One more step is necessary as part of the incubating process. You can't possess what you can't see. You must say what you see. We don't create alone and because we co-create, we never speak alone. We are either speaking with the voice of the Lord in us, or we are speaking with the enemy's voice. We repeat what we hear. Faith comes by hearing—hearing the Word of God He speaks to us, not what the enemy says. What we see is what we say and what we possess.

Words hold energy; therefore they are a living, breathing substance in the atmosphere that carry positive or negative charges of energy. Once spoken into the atmosphere, those positive or negatively charged packets of energy become a greater force of energy because like energies are attracted to them.

The same substance of energy will cause synergy to take place: the cooperative action of two or more like substances, causing multiplication and even acceleration. Remember, energy attracts like energy. The attractive energies from your words always hold a connection to where the energy originated from—out of your mouth from the inside of your heart. Deuteronomy 28:2 says, "And all these blessings shall come on thee, and overtake thee, if thou shalt hearken unto the voice of the LORD thy God" makes sense. It says in Deuteronomy 28:1 that "it shall come to pass." The blessings shall come on you and overtake you. This is understandable when you think in terms of having awareness that words are energy.

This is also why it is important to write the vision as talked about in Habakkuk 2: 2, "And the LORD answered me, and said, Write the vision, and make it plain upon tables, that he may run that readeth it." It is important to make the vision clear and to have that in writing to refer back to when the enemy wants to come against destroying it. It isn't a question of if he will want to destroy it but when and for how long he will come at you. The clearer you make the picture the better for like energy to cause attraction to have synergy.

The Bible says the opposite is also true for curses. Deuteronomy 28:15 says, "But it shall come to pass, if thou wilt not hearken unto the voice of the LORD thy God, to observe to do all his commandments and his statutes which I command thee this day; that all these curses shall come upon thee, and overtake thee." Be careful what you consistently focus on, observe carefully, or watch closely with continued persistence.

I believe this is what King David understood about worshiping and praising God. He praised Him when things were bad. By doing that he was creating a shift or an overtaking of negative energy with positive energy from God. This is why I believe the word tells us to praise and worship Him when all hell is breaking loose in our lives. It has to do more with energies taking over the atmosphere around your life and converting them from negative energy to positive energy. Like attracts like causing multiplied energy.

We Must Take the Reins

This is meant to give you knowledge so you can understand what to do, what not to do, and how to get what you really want in your life. Life doesn't need to run us any longer. We must take the reins and run life based upon awareness and accurate perception of what is happening to us, making necessary changes to our thinking. It starts with our thoughts.

Always remember, the greater power of energy is in the positive thoughts because they can always create something brand new. Understanding how your enemy tricks you is critical. Perhaps you have had an entire lifetime of wrong programming. It is never too late and never impossible to change your thinking (no matter your age or how big a challenge you are facing). Applying positive thoughts to your thinking can alter those negative programs. You have to know, be aware, and make a conscious effort to apply positive thoughts to your life. A miraculous change will take place. This is why Proverbs 4:23 says to, "Keep thy heart with all diligence; for out of it are the issues of life." Our issues we like to talk about so much are coming out of our own heart.

It is normal for you to have faith in your heart and doubt in your head at the same time. When you doubt in your mind that does not mean you have doubt in your heart. You control them remaining separate within you. It depends totally up on what you do with your mind's thoughts of doubt and unbelief. Do not brood upon them. Know where they are coming from and kick them out of your mind. If you don't they will travel to connect in your heart.

Jesus never said a word about doubting of the mind. He said not to doubt in the heart. Mark 11:23 says, "For verily I say unto you, That whosoever shall say unto this mountain, Be thou removed, and be thou cast into the sea; and shall not doubt in his heart, but shall believe that those things which he saith shall come to pass; he shall have whatsoever he saith."

Our mind has eyes to see what is physically present at the moment. Our heart has no eyes for what is seen physically but it does have spiritual eyes to look at what is unseen. Seeing with your spiritual eyes is vital for calling things that are not visible, as though they were. "As though they were" refers to the period of time in the incubator where you focus on what you see with your spiritual eyes and speak with your mouth what you see, until you see it with your physical eyes. Romans 4:17b says, "calleth those things which be not as though they were."

Our lives are constantly moving from the invisible to the visible. Second Corinthians 5:7 tells us this plainly: "For we walk by faith, not by sight." The Lord knows the enemy will access your mind with doubt and unbelief. What we don't understand is that we give the access to our heart for the doubt and unbelief by focusing too long and hard upon them. Then those images make a connection to our heart and cancel the positive thoughts we have been incubating. If you doubt anything, doubt your doubts and believe in what's in your incubator. Believe in your original images—that is required to remain hopeful. Keep your hope active. Don't turn your hope off.

This is what Paul talks about when he says, "Fight the good fight of the faith; lay hold of the eternal life to which you were summoned and [for which] you confessed the good confession [of faith] before many witnesses" (1 Timothy 6:12, AMP)." Notice that both laying hold to keep what is in your incubator and confessing with your mouth what you see inside are both required conditions. You will lead your heart in this fight to claim victory.

Don't Doubt your Faith

Don't doubt the word of God. Don't doubt your faith, the pictures you see with your spiritual eyes. Doubt the thoughts of doubt that come into your head and ignore what you do not see (for the moment) with your physical eyes. What I am confessing with my mouth by faith will work with doubt coming to my head. I know this to be true in my personal life.

Back when I didn't know what I now know, I realize I was fighting doubt. Even when things showed up that I had believed for—I was shocked when they did. I didn't realize that by refusing to think of the doubt and beliefs coming to my mind, I wasn't allowing a heart to head connection. If I would have dwelt on those thoughts with consistent focus, my heart would have taken agreement with them. You agree when you harmonize with thoughts to long. Those images would have canceled the images that I had in my heart of what I was hoping for.

Never forget that you are agreeing with the Holy Spirit. He is in your heart, helping to incubate what you see. When your spirit agrees with the word of God that is planted in your heart, the Holy Spirit helps you to incubate the thing you are hoping for. You then have two agreeing for what you ask for and it will come to pass. Matthew 18:19-20 says, "Again I say unto you, That if two of you shall agree on earth as touching any thing that they shall ask, it shall be done for them of my Father which is in heaven. For where two or three are gathered together in my name, there am I in the midst of them." The Holy Spirit is a person and you are a person. Your soul comes into agreement with your spirit and the Holy Spirit makes three that agree.

You must keep in harmony and synergy to cause a physical form to be created from what you observe with the eyes of your heart. Hold fast to what you desire. Hope has pictures and pictures are the substance incubating in your heart. In the beginning, it has nothing to do with what you see with your physical eyes. Yes, it can be normal when you don't see your healing and don't feel it either. It can be considered normal when you don't see finances at first. Understand which eyes you're starting with. Don't go into natural human reasoning. Hebrews 11:6 says, "But without faith it is impossible to please him: for he that cometh to God must believe that he is, and that he is a rewarder of them that diligently seek him." Faith requires a belief in God for what you are hoping to change in your life for the better.

We see lack because we have been taught how to see it. There is no lack in God. When you focus on what you may lack, you give power to it. Observe what you want to bring into your life. By focusing on the need, we allow the substance of energy to remain with us, causing the need to remain with us as well. We must change energies to cause a new thing to form to replace an old thing.

New thought images = new energy substance = transformation of the new image into a physical form.

We were created with all the tools necessary to produce things. The process of producing is a constant thing that is happening in us. We are a production factory designed to multiply things on the earth. Everything produced on the earth comes through mankind.

Chapter 19

You are a Generator

Mankind is also a generator. A generator converts one form of energy into another form of energy. The seed is the word God has shown you. The soil is man's heart. The way we plant is by seeing images from the word, staying focused on them, and believing on those thoughts. Then you say what you heard from the word so you can move it from the inside to the outside of you. Just like a farmer, in due season you shall see fruit.

You are a conductor of energy. Your body is made up of seventy percent water. Water is a conductor of energy. The word is referred to as water. The water of the word comes to force production of the seeds planted in the soil of the heart.

In Luke 12:31 it says, "But rather seek ye the kingdom of God; and all these things shall be added unto you." Where is the kingdom of God? Most think it is outside of them—up in heaven, or in the cosmos somewhere. The kingdom of heaven is outside you, but where is the Kingdom of God? The Kingdom of God is inside you, in your heart. Let's look at how Jesus answered that question when asked by the Pharisees: "And when he (Jesus) was demanded of the Pharisees, when the kingdom of God should come, he answered them and said, The kingdom of God cometh not with observation: Neither shall they say, Lo here! or, lo there! for, behold, the kingdom of God is within you" (Luke 17:20-21, author parentheses).

You are a Production Factory

Matthew 21:43 even talks about the Kingdom of God inside of man being taken away for not producing fruit for the Lord's kingdom: "The kingdom of God shall be taken from you, and given to a nation bringing forth the fruits thereof." Thoughts equal images (seeds) that produce when watered. The production of the kingdom is inside of you. So how do we water the seed? By washing our thoughts with His word! This is the washing of the water of the word talked about in Ephesians 5:26: "That he might sanctify and cleanse it with the washing of water by the word." His word is the water going forth to produce what the seed holds.

You put pressure on the seed (the word), to produce by giving it the right climate inside of you and then by speaking into the atmosphere outside of you. That is how you can see what you say in the right season. Words spoken by faith will put pressure on circumstances you face. So when you believe in your heart, not allowing the doubt in your head to travel to your heart, the pictures incubating in your heart won't be canceled, and you shall have what you say.

Everything has its perfect time to manifest physically. The third chapter of Ecclesiastes tells us this. God orchestrates all manifestations into the whole. We are part of a bigger picture because we are each a part of the whole body of Christ.

Jesus taught in Mark 4:14 that the sower sows the word. That is pretty plain to mean that words produce things. You need to keep believing what your heart sees and confess from the heart with your mouth and it will manifest when it is time. Understand what can happen in your incubator. Think about what you are saying, it could be getting you into trouble.

Remember you are also a generator that converts present energy from one form to another. This means that positive energy can be converted into negative energy. Matthew 13:19 tells us that very thing: "When any one heareth the word of the kingdom, and understandeth it not, then cometh the wicked one, and catcheth away that which was sown in his heart. This is he which received seed by the way side." You must understand that the enemy is trying to steal the positive word pictures in your heart. He knows full well that if he doesn't steal—you will produce.

So in summary, the word of faith that comes by hearing (from the Kingdom of God) is spoken to you from the still small voice of the Holy Spirit inside your heart. The seed is the promise from God's word and a plan for your life. You see with the eyes of your heart and incubate (give it the right climate to develop and grow) by continuing to believe, trusting it to come, and saying what you see so it will manifest. You sow the words from one kingdom or the other. One kingdom is full of light and the other is full of darkness.

When you keep saying the words of faith, you are wording your faith. James 2:20 tells us that faith without works is dead. When you work your faith, more faith will be added to what you already have.

All energies of God hold light. He wants us to increase with his light. You are speaking with Him because we never speak alone. You are speaking with divine energy, which forces production of what the Word says. When divine energy is built up enough in you and has attracted enough outside of you, there is agreement with the kingdom, sufficient in proportion to cause a birthing of it—causing it to happen. You call things that are not as though they are and the voice of God inside you co-creates with you.

If you ever wonder what happened to your faith, check on what your mouth has been saying. Out of the abundance of the heart the mouth speaks. Luke 6:45 makes this very plain: "A good man out of the good treasure of his heart bringeth forth that which is good; and an evil man out of the evil treasure of his heart bringeth forth that which is evil: for of the abundance of the heart his mouth speaketh." Guard your heart. Proverbs 4:23 says, "Keep and guard your heart with all vigilance and above all that you guard, for out of it flow the springs of life" (AMP).

Remember that you are a spiritual generator, in operation every moment of every day. We harmonize with energies from one of two kingdoms. Jesus said we are cleansed by the Word (Ephesians 5:26). You being 70% water (which conducts energy), your enemy knows that if he can change the images you look at in your heart, he can stop them from manifesting and replace them with his thoughts. Those lies steal God's Word from inside your heart.

That is what is meant by the thorns in Luke 8:14: "And that which fell among thorns are they, which, when they have heard, go forth, and are choked with cares and riches and pleasures of this life, and bring no fruit to perfection." The thorns that grow in order to choke out the plans from the seed of God (the word pictures you are incubating) so they bear no fruit. Matthew 13:22 also warns us of this: "He also that received seed among the thorns is he that heareth the word; and the care of this world, and the deceitfulness of riches, choke the word, and he becometh unfruitful."

Satan's kingdom cannot steal the Word if you understand it and hold fast to it. Holding fast requires action—kicking thoughts of doubt and unbelief out of your mind. Also be advised that your enemy is very persistent and patient. Second Timothy 1:3 tells us to pray without ceasing. That is wisdom since the enemy never takes time off. Hebrews 3:6 tells us to, "hold fast the confidence and the rejoicing of the hope firm unto the end." We are also to hold fast the professing of our faith: "Let us hold fast the profession of our faith without wavering; (for he is faithful that promised)" (Hebrews 10:23).

Everything produces after its own kind. You put pressure on negative circumstances by speaking out the word of God, generating positive pressure. That is why God tells us to praise and worship Him in all circumstances. He knows that if we worry, we harmonize with negative energies of fear and we will bear its fruit. Now it makes even more sense why David was such a passionate worshiper of God. This is why we are to call God into remembrance of His word, and of His promises to us. We are harmonizing with His word by doing that. By speaking it out that energy is harmonizing around you.

Transforming the Mind

When we first start thinking with His divine energy, it begins to transform our mind. When we incubate those word images long enough, they cause the renewing of the mind. The word of God holds light capable of dispelling all dark thoughts coming from the negative kingdom. The more you dwell upon his word, the more light you contain. Once you build your faith, you must remember to keep your mouth from saying anything contrary to your pictures of faith. Continue to incubate the original images—words in your spirit.

Keep your focus with your spiritual eyes, not your natural eyes and speak as though you already have it, whether you believe for healing, finances, relationships or provision. We are using our spiritual eyes to see what our natural eyes cannot, until it manifests in the natural. Be careful what you say and listen to because you are seventy percent water and an energy conductor and converter. What we do affects not just us, but everyone around us as well. It is important who we keep company with. We can become infected and infect others as well. That may well be why God commands us to love others as we love ourselves. There is no energy stronger, or more powerful, then the energy of love.

Perception can Come from False Beliefs

Think about why your perception matters for everything in your life. Your perception can come from false beliefs. See why renewing your mind with the truth of the word of God is vital for everything you want to experience in your life. Positive thought energy breathes life into us when we meditate upon it and speak it to others. Our words matter! They speak light or darkness. They live on to affect us far into our future and even into future generations. Science is proving the truth found in the word all along. Words can wound us far greater than physical wounds.

Words hold damaging images that travel in our blood, throughout our system, causing chemical and neurological impulses that communicate toxic messages throughout our operating system nonstop. Over time, they can take their toll on us and deal us a lethal blow, from which we may not recover.

A law of the kingdom is that you shall speak what is in your heart. The power is in the tongue. The problem is we don't always believe what we're supposed to say. The power of life and death is in the tongue. Proverbs 4:20 says, "My son, attend to my words; incline thine ear unto my sayings." When pressure hits, whatever is in your heart is going to come out of your mouth. Whatever is stored in your heart produces what is in your life. Why? Your heart sends messages to every cell in your body, not just your brain. Those messages will produce fruits of blessings or curses. This is a law of the Kingdom of God. We speak law unto ourselves and others every day.

Proverbs 4:23 says, "Keep thy heart with all diligence; for out of it are the issues of life." That word "keep" means "to guard." How do you guard your heart? Understand that you program it in three basic ways: by what you see, by what you hear, and by what you meditate on. Meditating in the Word means to give continued persistent thought over.

Meditation

The enemy has twisted meditation to be an exercise of thinking on nothing, and of allowing whatever comes into your mind to enter and stay. That is dangerous for us, as it allows the enemy to bring thoughts to our minds that we might think are from the Lord—thoughts the enemy has twisted just enough for us to be unaware they have a lie built into them, just as he did with Eve in the garden. That is not the purpose of meditation as God intended. He told us to meditate upon His word for that reason. Meditating on truth from the word will always bring light into your body. As thoughts come to you as you meditate, you must go back to the word to see if it lines up as truth. Then you can incubate those thoughts of true revelation.

Anything you allow yourself to see or hear has the potential to program what you believe. Your eyes and ears are the gates to your body and soul. Your soul, which is your mind, affects the things stored in your heart by changing what you believe. Beliefs are altered by our thinking processes. It always comes down to the basic foundation being: as a man thinks, he becomes. This is a law of the kingdom. This law works exactly the same way for God as it does for us.

It is a law to guard our heart from thoughts that oppose what the Word says. All kingdoms have laws by which they are governed. You operate the law of the kingdom from inside yourself, by your words. You create life or death by what you say because of the law.

Most people don't know the laws or how they operate, nor do they know their rights. The enemy gets us to operate in a way that brings judgment upon us. Too many of us remain ignorant of our rights, allowing the enemy to turn the power we possess against us.

We curse ourselves with the words we speak because they are not truly our words, but they are the words the enemy originally spoke into our minds. We agree with those words. Next, they became planted in the soil of our heart to produce what we say. Meantime, our enemy sits in the dark and we don't even see what he's doing in us. Proverbs 4:19 tells us: "The way of the wicked is as darkness: they know not at what they stumble." We don't know how we stumble in the darkness. We need the light of the word to expose the dastardly deeds of the enemy.

If you really want to guard your heart, you must be aware of what enters your eye gate and ear gate and what you focus on in your thinking. This is why Proverbs 4:24 tells us to put away false and dishonest speech and to put contrary talk far from us. Contrary talk is walk that is contrary to what God says. Proverbs tells us what the law of the Kingdom of God should produce in our lives: "My son, attend to my words; incline thine ear unto my sayings. Let them not depart from thine eyes; keep them in the midst of thine heart. For they are life unto those that find them, and health to all their flesh" (Proverbs 4:20-22). Our words should produce life and health in our bodies. Proverbs 4:25 says we are to let our eyes look right.

For those of you who think you can watch something and then stop thinking about it, you are ignorant of how your non-conscious mind works. Earlier we explored how the non-conscious mind processes and stores information at the rate of 40 million bits per second. Our conscious mind can only process 40 bits of information per second. Whatever you see gets stored in your non-conscious mind, to be retrieved by your conscience mind at any time. Beliefs are formed when enough similar information is acquired.

The amygdala in our brain searches for matches from stored information like a library. Information coming through our five senses enters and the data is put into the library. This means that all the enemy has to do is speak something through another person to cause you to react to a false belief stored in your non-conscious mind. This causes you to speak and act out what you believe. We don't always understand why we believe what we do because the matched information isn't always accurately perceived and isn't always accurately matched. You will meditate on what you see and what you hear, either consciously or non-consciously.

You want to speak from springs of living water that flow from your heart. If you are having thoughts of never being able to change your life, you have just heard the enemy speak. Nothing is impossible with God because of the way He created us. Nothing is too big and it is never too late. Do not miss the biggest point of all of this—the word of God is the superpower of the universe. Your enemy is rendered powerless, not by your words, but by the words of the Lord. When you speak His word, He is speaking with you. Remember, we said that we never speak alone. We speak stored beliefs from our hearts that originated as a thought from one of two kingdoms.

You are an Heir but don't Speak

Think of it this way. Prince Charles is heir to the throne of England. He was born into the inheritance of the Kingdom of England. If someone kidnapped Prince Charles and he was subjected to trauma resulting in amnesia, does that change the fact that he is still an heir to the kingdom? No, but as long as he has amnesia he will not know how to speak or act like a prince. He will not know he has any authority to change his condition. But if he came out of his amnesia and became aware again of his true identity, do you think it would take him very long to change his life—to start living like a prince? No, of course not! So it is with you as a son or daughter of the King in the Kingdom of God.

What if the princes' captors roughed him up, left him unrecognizable, and brainwashed him into thinking he was a commoner? They tell him who he is but he doesn't believe it because of what he heard and suffered while kidnapped. He never tells anyone in England who he really is. With his appearance now unrecognizable, brainwashed from believing he was a prince, do you think the members of Parliament will allow him the privileges worthy of a prince? Does he or does he not still have those privileges? Would it do him any good to have the queen restore his position if he continues to keep his identity to himself and act like a commoner?

What do you think he would have to do to change his life back into that of a prince, with full privileges in the kingdom? He would have to believe in his heart that he is the prince and begin to speak and act as the prince. He must exercise his authority to operate the laws of the kingdom in order to experience the privileges afforded to him by the kingdom. Does he have to go to his mother, the queen, to ask her to speak for him if she dies and is made king? Of course not! In his new position as king, can he do anything that goes against the laws of England without opposition? No.

So it is with you when, as a son or daughter in the Kingdom of God, you walk around with either amnesia, brainwashed or with your identity marred—not knowing who you really are. You can't get the law to work for you when you don't believe who you are. Satan has programmed you to believe that he is the ruler and he has stolen the words and the law and kept them hidden from you. He has caused you to believe that everything bad that has happened in your life has been God's punishment for doing wrong. That is why his name is Satan, the master deceiver.

Make no mistake about it, as quick as Prince Charles remembers who he is, he will begin to operate with all the privileges of the kingdom and you, like him, can begin to change your life at any age no matter how much you have done wrong. You need to spend time finding your identity and learning how to operate with the laws of the kingdom. You have the authority but you must know how to use it.

James 3 says that if you stumble, it is due to a problem in the way you are operating the laws of the kingdom. The laws are operating against you instead of for you, due to your lack of knowledge. When you understand that, you are able to keep your whole body in check. You are the pilot of your life. Your heart directs where you go in life, like a rudder on a ship, and like a bit in a horse's mouth. What comes out of your mouth speaks your heart and gives you power over your life. Jesus died and went to hell to get the keys to the earth realm that Satan stole from Adam. The authority he regained has been given to you to empower you to take back your life.

You operate just like God because you are created in His image and likeness. If your heart is perverse, your tongue will be a fire, infecting your whole body. You must understand that the devil is coming for your words. He is always looking for access to affect what's in your heart, knowing you will speak life or death unto yourself and others.

Careful: You Get What you Say

A woman told this story about herself on talk radio. She said she had a dream from the Lord, warning her that she would give birth to a baby that would be retarded. She said she believed the Lord was preparing her ahead of time. The baby was born normal, but here's what came out of her own mouth at the birth: "No, the baby was suppose to be born retarded." What happened? She believed the baby was supposed to be born retarded and because she agreed with that lie, in eight months the baby developed the symptoms of being retarded.

First of all, the Lord would not give anyone a dream telling them their baby is going to be born retarded. It was a lie. The woman believed the lie of the enemy, confessed it with her mouth and released it to happen. She released the law into that situation that results in you having what you say.

This is why it is so important to know what the Word of God says. The systems of the world are cursed, but the keys (words) of the kingdom are inside you that overcome the world system. Greater is He that is in us, then he who is the world (1 John 4:4).

We cannot pray to God, expecting Him to do it without us. God only has access into this earth through us. He gave this earth to mankind to take dominion. We hold the keys that give us the authority to bind and loose on earth what comes into our lives. This is done by our words. Let's look at what Hebrews 4:12 says, "For the word of God is quick, and powerful, and sharper than any two edged sword, piercing even to the dividing asunder of soul and spirit, and of the joints and marrow, and is a discerner of the thoughts and intents of the heart." The word of God is alive and full of power, making it active, operational, energizing and effective at all times. When we speak, our words contain energy to bless or curse our bodies and even the air we breathe, filling our environment with life or death.

Low on Energy - Check your Thinking and Speaking

Do you want to change things in your life? The first place to look is inside your heart. How can you do that? You start by paying attention to what you're saying. If your words are negative, they are depleting your energy. If you start paying attention to your body, you will notice you are low on energy. You are in survival mode, and chances are, you feel like life is running you.

It takes positive energy to increase our energy and to create positive things in our lives. Positive energies create life, while negative energies remove the life from us. How do you change what you speak? Start by operating the law that says to guard your heart.

Next, you have to change false beliefs. Why? Anyone who speaks a lot of negative has a belief system supporting the negative thoughts they speak. Negative thoughts are false beliefs. What makes me say that? Negative thoughts hold negative energy and all negative thoughts come from the kingdom of darkness. There is no truth that comes from the kingdom of darkness. Truth can only be found in the word of God. When you feel like you have low energy, check your thinking and speaking.

So as you reexamine what you believe, you need to go to the Word to find out if it is truth. If you find that it is false, replace that belief with truth from the Word. Positive energy, or to say it another way, positive natures that we feel and express as positive thoughts, emotions, feelings, and attitudes originate in the heart. Negative thought originates in the mind and looks for agreement with you to make a connection in your heart.

The problem starts for believers when they don't look for the promises in the word that apply to their problems. Even if they do look, if they do not know their rights and are ignorant of how to govern the laws of the kingdom of God in their life, they have just as bad a problem.

When you gave your heart and life to the Lord, you entered the Kingdom of God. You became a citizen of the Kingdom of God. You became an heir to everything the kingdom holds—every promise written in the book is yours, due to the condition of your heart. What you allow to take root inside your heart determines what you receive as your fruit. You incubate, generate, and produce from those seeds that take root in your heart, because those trees bear fruit by what comes out of your mouth.

Chapter 20

Trust Keeps Faith Incubating

The definitions of trust are: 1) confident expectation of something; hope, 2) a person on whom or thing on which one relies, God is my trust or 3) confidence in the certainty of future payment for property or goods received. We learn to trust through experiences. Considering how many of those experiences we've had that are negative, we have learned to put our trust in many false perceptions.

How many of us have had broken trust in your life? Even when we've forgiven the person, it took time to trust again. Trust takes time to develop. Unfortunately, we can have confident expectation for the negative things that could potentially come into our lives from habitually dwelling on negative possibilities. We all have experienced disappointment, hurt, and failures in our lives. Our ability to trust comes from how we perceive what we have experienced in life.

How many of us have had a confident expectation for something good to happen in our lives and it didn't, or the opposite happened? After enough failures, we end up looking for something bad to happen instead of good. We end up trusting in the negative thoughts because we've learned all too well to believe the false perceptions. You might ask how it is a false perception? It's a false perception of your life as it could or should be. The true perception of who you really are is acquired by learning to internalize the thoughts from the Holy Spirit, not from your enemy.

In chapter 15, we said that true perception requires seeing something inside you that wants to be brought into existence outside of you. Thoughts and beliefs are invisible motion within us. We can't see them with our five senses until we paint them. What you perceive within yourself you must put onto a canvas so you can see it with your physical senses. The biggest way we paint perception is with the brush of words. This is how you get others to view your perception, to see things the way you see them, so they can experience what you are experiencing. This is why we have to speak what we "want" to see by faith.

We also said that words send out images. God is looking for our perceptions to match the images that He put within us. When we see ourselves as God sees us, we then have an optical fusion. When two images join they become one perception and the two become one.

Holy Spirit and Synergy

Mark Chironna, in a series called *The Promise of Favor*, said that the Holy Spirit on the inside of you is there to create synergy. Synergy is the cooperative action of two or more substances. You are made up of substance and He is all substances. The definition of synergy is: to increase the activity of (a substance). Synergy basically means that there is divine grace coupled with human activity that releases incredible power. In other words, the combined work of divine grace and human activity releases a power beyond us. The whole is greater than the sum of the parts. The major component to synergy with the Holy Spirit is trust.

We might think the major component is faith. He is the spirit of faith. You don't have to get faith, faith comes. We are told to trust Him in Proverbs 3:5, "Trust in the LORD with "all" thine heart; and lean not unto thine own understanding." Trusting the Lord is developed. Trust requires that you get to know Him and that requires faith and patience. He is the substance of all things hoped for and the evidence of what's unseen.

Just because we receive the Holy Spirit doesn't mean that we are aware and wise enough to know exactly what the spirit is saying to us in every situation. That is developed in time. You have to learn his ways, and how he thinks about you, so as to develop trust in Him. Somehow we get this false idea, after we give our heart to the Lord, that we now should have a "blind" trust in God for every great and wonderful thing. Trust is not blind, it is developed in a relationship. The enemy wants you to have a blind trust because that will keep you blind to what God says about what you are going through.

God wants you to learn his ways and be developed into his image and the conversation for learning is done with the Holy Spirit on the inside of you. He provides us comfort and guides your thoughts on how to replace false perceptions with truth from the Word. We learn to trust what comes from the communication in our hearts to form perceptions that are true.

Now if you consider this in light of how you process your thoughts. Would you not agree that the enemy goes to work immediately and consistently on getting you to believe that a relationship with the Holy Spirit doesn't need to be developed? Instead, he probably says something like this in your head, "I thought I could believe in you God. You didn't take care of that for me. How could a good God allow this to happen? I can't trust Him." (Remember, your enemy sounds like you.)

Because faith comes by hearing and hearing by the word of God, we've got to learn how to hear God. Faith is the substance of things hoped for and that substance comes by hearing. We learn to trust, or learn not to trust, in everything we hear but do we always hear what's true? Do we always believe what's true? What thoughts we hear and believe, we act out in our lives.

Faith comes by hearing and faith is a substance that has been sent to you to hope in. The substance contains a picture of what you hope for. You put that into your incubator to grow and all is well to start with. Now the enemy comes along with doubt and unbelief in your head and uses your previous history of false perceptions to plead his case with you. So this debate commences inside your head. You need to deal with that inner critic. How long you can endure that attack from him will determine how strong your confidence is for that which you hope. What determines the strength of your confidence is based on how strong your trust is in the Lord.

If you remember at the beginning of this chapter we said that trust was "confident expectation" of something, like hope. Hebrews 10:22-23 says this about faith, "Let us draw near with *a true heart in full assurance of faith*, having our hearts sprinkled from an evil conscience, and *our bodies washed with pure water*. (The water is the word of God) Let us *hold fast the profession of our faith without wavering*; (for he is faithful that promised;) and in verse 35, "*Cast not away therefore your confidence,* which *hath great recompense of reward.*" (Author Notations)

Your reward comes when you have trusted in the Lord for what He said He would do when you heard His promise to you. This revelation of His truth to you has revealed a substance to you, for you to <u>*trust*</u> in, to incubate by <u>*faith,*</u> and to agree with, or come into <u>*alignment*</u> with in order for that substance to manifest in your life.

But let's take note of something else in verse 36 of Hebrews 10. "For ye *have need of patience*, that, after ye have done the will of God, ye might receive the promise." He tells us that we need patience. You will only be able to keep your hope substance incubating with confident expectation and patience, if you "trust" in the Lord for the word you heard. We war with the weapons of His word against our enemy. His word is the only word that renders the enemy powerless.

Isaiah 26:3 tells us, "Thou wilt keep him in perfect peace, whose *mind is stayed on thee: because he trusteth in thee.*" One of the tactics of the enemy is fear. Fear has torment. We need to realize that when fear wants to attack us, we need to deal with it. Switch on your positive control system and begin to speak everything opposite to that fear. We need to stay the mind of our head with the mind of our heart where thee (Holy Spirit) is located. We have to keep that substance (images of hope) in our incubator in place, by using the Word against what the fear is saying to us in our head.

The enemy is going to bring up your past history of false perceptions, failures, and bad experiences for only one reason. He's showing you images from your past so you will put your trust in what has happened before that didn't work. If you take his bait, this causes an exchange of substance (images) in your heart. If he is successful in getting you to trust in what you've already seen before, that is the opposite of what you heard from God, he knows you will abort the baby growing in your incubator of faith. Learning to trust in God by faith that comes to you must be developed. Trusting in God comes by developing a relationship with Him. This takes time spent with Him.

Synergy with the Holy Spirit inside of you brings you into alignment with all things necessary for everything to fall into place. Fusion is what causes alignment. Fusion is the coming together of two or more entities to form something much heavier that releases a great deal of energy that could not be released otherwise. Synergy requires alignment, alignment brings fusion. The weight of God is called His glory. When the energy of your spirit (your positive control system) is in alignment with the energy of God it causes a power of energy release that is greater than the sum of the parts. This is the Holy Spirit and your spirit co-creating as one.

We must trust in Him first, then have faith, then come into alignment with the Holy Spirit to cause a fusion that will bring about a great reward. If we don't have enough trust in Him that is no problem. He always meets us where we need to start, or restart, even if that is for the ten thousandth and one time. He never stops meeting us if we seek Him first. He never leaves us nor forsakes us.

Matthew 6:33 says, "But seek ye first the kingdom of God, and his righteousness; and all these things shall be added unto you." We seek the kingdom of God first to develop a relationship with Him to find out who He says we are. In that relationship He reveals things about us to us; that are hidden in us for us. This relationship develops our trust in Him and His trust in us. He reveals things to us when He can trust us.. Ps 37:4 says, "Delight thyself also in the LORD: and he shall give thee the desires of thine heart."

Is it possible that we have been too hard on ourselves and others to believe that something didn't happen because someone didn't have enough faith? I know this to true in my life. I thought I had enough faith for something and couldn't understand why it didn't happen. The Lord had to deal with me about my level of trust in Him and reveal to me what it can do to my faith.

Without a firm trust in God your hope can become compromised. When your hope becomes compromised, your faith is shattered.

When your faith is shattered, the substance of things hoped for are gone. Is it becoming clearer to you how important trust needs to be.

This is the reason 1 Timothy 1:19 talks about your faith being shipwrecked. "Holding fast to faith ([b]that leaning of the entire human personality on God *in absolute trust and confidence*) and having a good (clear) conscience. By rejecting and thrusting from them [their conscience], some individuals have made shipwreck of their faith." (AMP)

Let me illustrate this to you in my own life. Our earthly father is suppose to be an example of our heavenly father. This was what God intended. The father in the home is to take the position and is the authority in the home, *as unto Christ*. Please notice the part that says "as unto Christ". This is spoken of in 1 Corinthians 11:3, "But I would have you know, that *the head of every man is Christ*; and the head of the woman is the man; and *the head of Christ is God*."

My Earthly Father and Abba Father

I did not have a godly father. And even if he were godly, he would not have been exempt from what I'm about to explain to you. As parents we recycle the behaviors that were taught to us from our parent's. We need to realize this, so we don't condemn each other for wrong toxic behaviors that we have repeated due to lack of knowledge. The kingdom of our enemy works hard to program toxic thoughts from one generation to the next.

My earthly father gave me good gifts. I cannot judge his motivation behind the gift giving. My parents were divorced when I was three years old. I didn't get to see my father every week. He may have given gifts to me out of guilt or he may have genuinely wanted to give them. But whenever Christmas, or my birthday would be coming, he would ask me what I wanted. I would be excited to ask him for some big gift I had in mind months before Christmas or my birthday would show up. I usually got one gift because my birthday is close to Christmas.

You see, my father loved to tease me for months before my birthday. He would say things that led me to believe I might be getting what I asked for. But then he'd turn around and say things with a smile on his face that led me to doubt I would get it. He played the same game of teasing me each birthday, even as an adult. I'm telling you he loved to tease, not just me, but others as well.

There is an extremely large water tower that you see from the freeway in Milwaukee, Wisconsin. On several occasions when passing that water tower my dad had Norby (his grandson, my son) in the car with him. Starting at around the age of six years old he told Norby that he was going to hang him up from that water tower with his belt. Even though he was smiling when he said it to him, at the age of six or seven, Norby believed what he said. Norby continued to believe it until around 9 years of age. I never knew this story until he finally figured out his grandpa wasn't serious. Until that time he said it use to scare him spit-less. My dad just figured that everybody else should have as much fun being teased as he enjoyed doing the teasing. I don't know if teasing is ever fun when you are on the receiving end.

Now, I'm not even talking about malicious teasing, which is worse. I'm talking about the kind of teasing that I'm sure most all of us have done. It's the kind of thing that we say when we don't think we mean what we just said and we say; "I was just kidding." We think it is harmless when we are doing it but we need to rethink why we are saying it in the first place. I myself haven't given too much thought to this teasing from my dad before now. In fact, nothing about this ever came to light until writing this book. I needed the transformation of this revelation.

Even though in most of the cases he ended up giving me the gift that I asked for, I had already given up all hope of getting it. Here is what this behavior built on the inside of me. It has messed up my firm ability to trust in what the Holy Spirit reveals to me and the promises of God found in His word.

It taught me to control the emotions of excitement, joy, and fun that comes with a child like confident expectation of receiving gifts. To say that another way, I learned how to carefully *not get my hopes up* because I learned it felt better to be "safe than sorry" to not place my trust in receiving. This meant I didn't trust the gift giver to mean what he said.

This caused my imagination to diminish for a substance I had put my hope in. In other words, my incubator kept losing babies that I couldn't hold until they were ready to birth. My ability to imagine was stifled because I didn't want my hopes dashed. It felt better to not hope. Am I talking to anyone else reading this? Your imagination involves seeing images of what you hope in. Over time I simply could not trust my earthly father for what I was asking and didn't trust what he said.

This didn't just involve gifts because it carried over into promises he gave me of coming to visit me, taking me places, doing things with me, etc. This trust issue automatically transferred to my lack of trust in my heavenly Father. It caused me to question what I was hearing from Him. It caused me to not get my hopes up for what He was telling me.

In the case with my Dad, he asked me on one hand what I wanted and on the other hand by teasing me, he told me to not expect it. It wasn't the same excitement for me even when I would get what I had given up hope of getting. This also affected my ability to ask. I either wouldn't ask or I would make sure I asked for something small enough. By asking smaller, the chances were greater I might receive what I asked. Over time it felt more comfortable emotionally for me to not hope for too much. Who taught me how to put emotional controls upon positive natures that reside within me? Without hesitation, most would answer by saying it was my dad. No, I realize my dad didn't know who was talking through him. The enemy programs our thoughts to cause our hearts to believe the opposite of what God says.

When our trust becomes stronger in the Lord, what you have faith for (which is the substance of things hoped for) cannot be dashed. This breach of trust is happening in the heart, where all substances for hope incubate through the act of faith. Guard your heart with all diligence from the toxic thoughts of your enemy.

I have forgiven my dad. How can I not forgive him and then ask my son to forgive me because I am sure I have repeated many more bad behaviors toward him. None of us are exempt but all of us can begin a new with understanding.

Our heavenly Father never teases us with any word of promise. To tease by definition means to provoke or disturb a person by persistent petty annoyances. God will never reveal one thing to us that lines up with His word, and do another, unless we refuse to believe. His word is truth. God speaks no promise that doesn't carry the full power of His light and the full potential of all possibilities to those who believe Him to bring it to pass.

Blessings from Waiting & Trusting

The blessings that come from learning to trust our heavenly Father are abundant. Take a look at a few scriptures. Isaiah 55:11 tells us how certain the word of the Lord is; "So shall my word be that goeth forth out of my mouth: *it shall not return unto me void,* but *it shall accomplish that which I please,* and it shall prosper in the thing whereto I sent it."

He speaks of His spoken promises in His word and how certain those promises are for us in 2 Corinthians 1:20; "For all the promises of God in him are yea, and in him Amen, unto the glory of God by us."

We are blessed if we learn to trust Him. See Psalm 34:8, "O taste and see that the LORD is good: blessed is the man that trusteth in him."

Psalm 40: 4: "Blessed is that man that maketh the LORD his trust, and respecteth not the proud, nor such as turn aside to lies."

Psalm 56:11: "In God have I put my trust: I will not be afraid what man can do unto me."

Psalm 118:8; "It is better to trust in the LORD than to put confidence in man."

Proverbs 29:25, "The fear of man bringeth a snare: but whoso putteth his trust in the LORD shall be safe."

Jeremiah 17:7, "Blessed is the man that trusteth in the LORD, and whose hope the LORD is."

Last but not least we will need to realize that we have to wait upon the Lord for what we are trusting. God has a time for all things. Everything that happens is part of a bigger picture that only God sees. He shows us puzzle pieces and gives us a word or two (I would love a paragraph or a chapter please) as we keep walking with Him.

We say we would like to know more but there is a problem that the Lord has with us if He tells us too much. First, if He told us what we were to do as our ultimate assignment for our lives, we would never believe He was talking about us. Also, He can't tell us everything at once because when He tells us, then our enemy hears also and will try to mess up the plan God has for you. Which is why we need to trust Him with our lives.

Psalm 112:7 declares we should have no fear of evil when we trust in our heart. "He shall not be afraid of evil tidings; his heart is firmly fixed, trusting (leaning on and being confident) in the Lord." (AMP) "He shall not be afraid of evil tidings: his heart is fixed, trusting in the LORD." He strengthens our heart by waiting in Psalm 27:14, "Wait on the LORD: be of good courage, and he shall strengthen thine heart: wait, I say, on the LORD." He gives us expectation for it to come in Psalm 62:5, "My soul, wait thou only upon God; for my expectation is from him." He shall exalt us to inherit that which we wait for in Psalm 37:34, "Wait on the LORD, and keep his way, and he shall exalt thee to inherit the land: when the wicked are cut off, thou shalt see it."

We need to develop a trust in God. He is the only one that can truly be trusted. It is essential to develop our faith. We need confident trust in Him, then faith, then alignment, then fusion and then comes our reward. We do this by getting a vision from Him, meditating upon it so as to get a clear picture of it (the clearer the better), write it down making it crystal clear in detail and then declare it with your voice. Don't give up, wait until you receive your reward.

The final best thought is this: "If ye then, being evil, know how to give good gifts unto your children, *how much more shall* your Father which is in heaven *give good things to them that ask him?*" (Matthew 7:11) That is how good God is to us! We learn this by seeking to know Him. Above all trust Him because you can!

Chapter 21

Be Transformed

First, for the greatest results, use the word of God to turbo-boost your positive control system. All positive emotions are good but for greater results overall, wash with the Word.

This book is the result of my own personal transformation. The Lord showed me what to write; leading me to the word of God, to biology, and to specific areas where both the Bible and biology matched up. I popped many qwiffs, my mind became renewed, and I have now become the message found in this book. I am beyond thankful to the Holy Spirit for bringing me the messages of revelation (Jesus, the word) from my Abba Father. All three working together as one are the reason for this book. I am changed by the light of revelation He has caused me to see. I love my heavenly Daddy more than I have words to express. He is and has always been faithful to me. I dedicate this to Him to work the same in you.

My point to saying that is this. If that happened to me as the Lord revealed many things about me to me, the very same thing can happen for you by using the knowledge and understanding found in this book that is full of His word and understanding.

It all started for me by faith. God told me over a year before I started to write that He wanted me to write a book. I couldn't observe myself as a writer. By the time the third prophecy was spoken to me, the last one followed by someone asking me point blank, "Have you started to write your book yet?" I knew the Lord was not giving up on me to unpack that hidden treasure He had put in me when He created me in His thoughts.

The same person who asked me about progress on my book is the same person who told me exactly what the book would be about. God is truly amazing when we allow Him to work in us and don't box Him in.

I remember thinking, "How in the world am I ever going to know what to write, let alone putting words and thoughts together that made sense?" Alone, I didn't have a clue of how or where to start. This whole thing has been done by faith in His word, as given to me, and putting my thoughts into action to begin. It got easier as I went along well past the twenty-one days. This is a testimony to what can be done if you allow the Lord to show you hidden treasures within you and to believe in His words to you.

This book, along with its workbook, is intended to become a tool to use to transform your thinking. As a new believer or mature believer, if we never stop seeking Him, He never stops revealing things to us. Use it along with its companion workbook called, **Think Well, Live Well Now Workbook**, the guide to your **21 Day Mind Boot Camp.** (For information go to: *http://www.thinkwelllivewellnow.com*) It gives you 21 days of daily study to work on that you can apply to your personal situations in your life. That can be for anything you want to transform in your life; healing, relationships, finances or whatever you are going through now. It will help you learn how to invest in the greatest gift you have been given. That gift is the hidden treasure on the inside of you waiting to be unpacked by you.

It can also be used as a discipleship tool for new believers. The workbook will teach you how and where to find the promises of God and how to apply them to your personal challenges in life to empower you to transform them. Use it along with a Strong's Concordance to find the words in Scripture you need to confess to change your circumstances and many more ideas daily. It doesn't matter what your situation, there are promises in His word that you can speak over your health, your finances, or any difficult situation in your life.

You can begin your personal or group transformation by committing to a 21 Day Mind Boot Camp. What do I mean? Just this; it takes twenty-one days (if you remember from the beginning of this book where it taught you about the trees in our brain), to "regrow" branches. It takes twenty-one days to cause a physical change in our brain. That is why it is important to not miss a single day of mind boot camp for the first twenty-one days. If you do, immediately pick it back up and keep going. (Go back to the chapter entitled Invisible Thoughts Grow Trees, sub-section 21 days to grow new trees (pg. 31), to reread about what this process of renewing your mind does inside the brain so you know how important it is to do certain things when they will crop up in your thoughts.)

I am calling the start up a 21 Day Mind Boot Camp because it can feel like a boot camp trying to take control of your thoughts. When you enroll in the armed services they prepare you in boot camp to change your habits to conquer the enemy. Similarly, you are training to do what it takes to win the war.

Much like war, which at this writing we are still fighting in Afghanistan, most of the time you don't take all the territory in a day or a week. It is a consistent strategy of applying winning principles on a daily basis. The enemy doesn't post a sign that says; "No fighting today, will resume next week." We think that is laughable. Yet this is how we approach our enemy. I assure you he will never put out a sign to stop for any moment in time.

Here is the important part of what you must do with thoughts beginning on day one of this 21 day mind boot camp. With every new thought or old thoughts you remember, if you hold it in your conscious thinking within a forty-eight hour time frame, that thought can be changed in your conscious anytime within that forty-eight hour period. That means if you change your beliefs that formed that thought within one hour, you are finished with that thought and can move on to others. Other thoughts may require forty-eight hours, and yet others you may not transform without repeating the process several times.

Remember, if you don't change it within forty-eight hours, it goes back into memory even stronger than when it came out. You will not be able to transform each and every thought within forty-eight hours, nor will you transform all thoughts within twenty-one days. Remember, this is boot camp. This prepares you to change how you move with your thoughts in the battle. After twenty-one days, new habits are forming. Keep going on but know it will get easier to do with practice. Being consistent is the key. Your enemy never stops being consistent. Do not condemn yourself. The Lord never condemns—your enemy does. God is more patient with us then we ever could be for ourselves.

Learning What and Who Love Is

If you are like the vast majority of people in this cursed world, you have experienced hurts, been wounded, and lack love. Love both for yourself and from others seems to be a thing most have negative thoughts about. How do I know that? Think about it with me. If God is love, what do you think the enemy has thrown at you all your life to snuff out? That is why love is a root issue in some ways no matter if it is a little, or a lot. This is where you will have to begin to make changes. You would say why must I start there? Let me explain why this is critical to your start.

To the greater degree you have been hurt, by the same measure, you are unable to give out love. You can't love others if you don't love yourself first. If you don't love yourself, you can't receive healing from God because God IS love. Love is the energy that you can't operate without. You were wired for love. You must engage the energy of love in order to make an effective, long lasting change on the inside. It is what connects you with the Holy Spirit in your heart, allowing congruency from your heart to your mind so you can harmonize and be in sync for change.

It is the positive nature that all other positive emotions grow from. All positive natures are housed within the one ultimate energetic power known as love (God).

The energy of love is what sustained Jesus through the cross and what it presented and love is what raised Christ from the dead. Love is also the powerful energy that Jesus took to go to hell and get the keys back from Satan to this earth so man once again would have dominion over it, through Christ. The Word says that love covers a multitude of sins. (Proverbs 10:12) It literally renders sin powerless of its energies over us and cancels them out. You could say that love is the superpower.

The other reason you need to start with love is that without being able to love yourself and others, your perception of God is automatically one of a hard taskmaster. The problem with that approach is, if you struggle to move forward in the activation of your positive control system, your enemy will always be able to block your progress. He will tell you things that to you will verify a lack of love from God towards you, as being the reason you can't change what you are trying to, or why you can't do something new because of all your previous attempts. It simply won't work long-term, no matter if it is healing, success or relationships, without fixing your love relationship with God.

The love of God has been (not will be) shed abroad in our hearts. You already have God's love inside you. Love is the energy all things are made from. The enemy has worked for a long time to blind you from that fact because he knows he's in trouble when you finally believe the truth. You were made in God's image and likeness. What is God's image and likeness? That is an easy answer once you see it. God is love! Love is His powerful energy and when seeds are planted from the original plant, you end up with a version of the original seed. Apple seeds produce apple trees with fruit of apples—not pears. Seeds hold images. The apple seed has an image of an apple tree in it; a pear seed holds the image of a pear.

You must see that because you are a seed from God. That means you are an image of God, that being the image of love. You are capable of all things you can ever imagine right now, if you will only believe. Why is imagining correctly so important? The image of the whole is in the seed. When you look at any seed, just like we learned earlier, every cell in your body is a picture of the whole, this is called fractal image, so it is with any seed of thought or idea. How you image that person, or thing, will be what it grows into eventually.

So if you have an image of yourself as not being able to love yourself or another, you can't produce what you want to change for the positive. You will keep having difficulty activating or keeping your positive control system engaged. Love is the energy or shall we think like this, love is the ultimate seed for which all other seeds come from. God is love who spoke everything into existence and it became what He spoke. That is what I mean when I say all other seeds came from the seed of love. This is why you must have the true perception of love in order to produce positive changes. When your beliefs in the heart hold more love, then your perceptions will also change. You will go from believing God has sent you a difficulty, into thanking God for allowing the difficulty so you would overcome it and be a threat to Satan instead of a victim of sin.

This is why I suggest you may need to start at the very beginning to understand how God feels about you. If that is the case, then start with this. Take this to heart by meditating on all these words that Love says you are, so as to transform your thinking.

I love this piece written and arranged by; Robert Critchley. It says so much about how our heavenly Father loves us beyond our comprehension. If you have anything less than the belief that God is good and loves you and always has your back, start meditating on these words.

My Child...

You may not know me, but I know everything about you
   ...Psalm 139:1

I know when you sit down and when you rise up
   ...Psalm 139:2

I am familiar with all your ways
   ...Psalm 139:3

Even the very hairs on your head are numbered
   ...Matthew 10:29-31

For you were made in my image
   ...Genesis 1:27

In me you live and move and have your being
...Acts 17:28

For you are my offspring
...Acts 17:28

I knew you even before you were conceived
...Jeremiah 1:4-5

I chose you when I planned creation
...Ephesians 1:11-12

You were not a mistake, for all your days are written in my book
...Psalm 139:15-16

I determined the exact time of your birth and where you would live
...Acts 17:26

You are fearfully and wonderfully made
...Psalm 139:14

I knit you together in your mother's womb
...Psalm 139:13

And brought you forth on the day you were born
...Psalm 71:6

I have been misrepresented by those who don't know me
...John 8:41-44

I am not distant and angry, but am the complete expression of love
...1 John 4:16

And it is my desire to lavish my love on you
...1 John 3:1

Simply because you are my child and I am your Father
...1 John 3:1

I offer you more than your earthly father ever could
...Matthew 7:11

For I am the perfect father
...Matthew 5:48

Every good gift that you receive comes from my hand
...James 1:17

For I am your provider and I meet all your needs
...Matthew 6:31-33

My plan for your future has always been filled with hope
...Jeremiah 29:11

Because I love you with an everlasting love
...Jeremiah 31:3

My thoughts toward you are countless as the sand on the seashore
...Psalms 139:17-18

I rejoice over you with singing
...Zephaniah 3:17

I will never stop doing good to you
...Jeremiah 32:40

For you are my treasured possession
...Exodus 19:5

I desire to establish you with all my heart and all my soul
...Jeremiah 32:41

And I want to show you great and marvelous things
...Jeremiah 33:3

If you seek me with all your heart, you will find me
...Deuteronomy 4:29

Delight in me and I will give you the desires of your heart
...Psalm 37:4

For it is I who gave you those desires
...Philippians 2:13

I am able to do more for you than you could possibly imagine
...Ephesians 3:20

For I am your greatest encourager
...2 Thessalonians 2:16-17

I am also the Father who comforts you in all your troubles
...2 Corinthians 1:3-4

When you are brokenhearted, I am close to you
...Psalm 34:18

As a shepherd carries a lamb, I have carried you close to my heart
...Isaiah 40:11

One day I will wipe away every tear from your eyes
...Revelation 21:3-4

And I'll take away all the pain you have suffered on this earth
...Revelation 21:3-4

I am your Father, and I love you even as I love my son, Jesus
...John 17:23

For in Jesus, my love for you is revealed
...John 17:26

He is the exact representation of my being
...Hebrews 1:3

He came to demonstrate that I am for you, not against you
...Romans 8:31

And to tell you that I am not counting your sins
...2 Corinthians 5:18-19

Jesus died so that you and I could be reconciled
...2 Corinthians 5:18-19

His death was the ultimate expression of my love for you
...1 John 4:10

I gave up everything I loved that I might gain your love
...Romans 8:31-32

If you receive the gift of my son Jesus, you receive me
...1 John 2:23

And nothing will ever separate you from my love again
...Romans 8:38-39

Come home and I'll throw the biggest party heaven has ever seen
Luke 15:7...

I have always been Father, and will always be Father
...Ephesians 3:14-15

My question is...Will you be my child?
...John 1:12-13

> *I am waiting for you*
> **...Luke 15:11-32**

Love, Your Dad. Almighty God

I want to confess this over you as a decree and proclamation.

You are a transformer, you are not a conformer, but a transformer and that just as the Word says, "do not conform to the pattern of this world but be transformed by the renewing of your mind." Be transformed by the Word. You will understand how to transform yourself. You will understand by the word of God and how it transforms even the things that are going on around you. It's not just for you but for those around you that you transform the atmosphere and the people around you by the Word that you speak. You are transformed and you are renewed by the washing of the water of the Word. This washing comes from your words. As the Lord washes you and you understand how His words washed over you and transformed you, you understand that your words have the same power to wash over others. You shall become the message of your transformation.

Lord I thank you for the words you have placed in this person's heart and in their spirit. Lord we say that those words come out because they are transformational. That this person whom you created in your image doesn't need to try and be like everyone else and doesn't need to fit the pattern of this world. But rather I call them transformed to become a transformer and that they operate in the transformational. Lord, just as caterpillars become butterflies, this person shall see the miraculous happen because of the words they speak. Because the words that are spoken are spirit and life and have become truth that they have realized in their own life. So Lord I thank you for this son or daughter of yours and I thank you for the transformer you have called them to be. In Jesus Name. Amen.

Make the decision *now* to enter a **21 Day Mind Boot Camp** of your own. Don't put it off. I see prophetically, 21 Day Mind Boot Camps on the internet. Develop your own groups of people for a 21 Day Mind Boot Camp, or do it with a friend or two. Hold each other up and accountable for your transformational changes. Share your testimonies and encourage one another. Be creative. Yes, it will take work on your part, but think of how much happier you can become by finding your purpose driven life. Have fun popping qwiffs to transform what has held you captive for far too long in your thoughts.

Change your thoughts and you will change your life. It's not what you look at that matters as much as what you see. Begin to see yourself different and you can transform into what you see. Remember, the way you see yourself is the way your enemy and others see you. You are a transmitter and receiver. Careful what you look at, and observe; you cause it to be.

I leave you with one fabulous thought. I wish I could say it is my quote but I can't. It is one of my favorite thoughts. It is a quote from Kim Clement who sings a song about it.

"You're somewhere in the future and you look much better than you look right now."

CPSIA information can be obtained at www.ICGtesting.com
Printed in the USA
LVOW062349080612

285265LV00001B/143/P